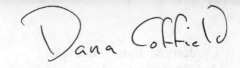

Carderock: Past and Present
A Climber's Guide

Prepared by

Selma I. Hanel

Mountaineering Section
Potomac Appalachian Trail Club
Washington D.C.
1990

Carderock: Past and Present
A Climber's Guide
Editor: Selma I. Hanel
Drawings: John C. Christian
Geology of the Area: John C. Reed, Jr.
Boulder Problems: Art Powell
Accident Analysis: Stuart Pregnall
Cover Drawing: Nori Eakin
Photo Reproduction: Wayne Firth
Photo Credits: As noted

Acknowledgments: Without the editors of *Up Rope* who
recorded Carderock's history, and without the active
climbers of today, this book would not be as complete.
Those who contributed memories and route descriptions are
thanked as well as those who climbed, scouted, and rated
routes; unfortunately, they are too numerous to mention
individually. James Eakin and Stuart Pregnall contributed
greatly by editing many drafts and answering endless
questions, and John Yanson assisted in the layout. The
writing of a guide to Carderock is difficult because so
many climbers have for years been putting up new routes
and it is often difficult to properly credit a first ascent or
to determine which name for a climb is the original.
Corrections may be sent to Editor, Carderock Guidebook,
PATC, 1718 N St. N.W., Washington D.C. 20036.
Proceeds from this guide book's sales will be used by the
PATC Mountaineering Section to continue its activities in
support of the local climbing community.

First edition
Potomac Appalachian Trail Club
1718 N Street, N.W., Washington, D.C. 20036

Library of Congress Catalog Card Number: 90-61742
ISBN 0-915746-40-9

Climbing is Dangerous

Rock climbing is dangerous. Proper techniques must be used to insure the safety of the climber and the belayer. This guidebook is for those competent in rockclimbing. Individuals who need instruction are encouraged to approach the local climbing schools and clubs.

Carderock has a high number of climbers. Soloing, or unroped climbing, can frequently be seen and it is courteous to do this in unpopulated sections where there is no danger to other climbers and belayers below.

In an emergency at Carderock and at Camp Lewis, the nearest telephone is located at the first parking lot when entering the park; dial 911 or the U.S. Park Police at 426-6600. At Boucher Rock, the nearest telephone is located at the private residences at the end of Balls Road.

Carderock: Past and Present
A Climber's Guide

List of Photos

Preface

Carderock is a unique natural resource located near the Nation's capital. It has a long history as a climbing area and today it offers the best local bouldering with easy access. Carderock's character is largely defined by it's history, and it is the purpose of this guide to provide a historic perspective to climbing at Carderock.

If the intent is to climb, the route descriptions will assist in finding the desired difficulty of climb. If the intent is to go to a less populated rock, to explore and to do "new" routes, this book provides directions to other cliffs and it is hoped that it will encourage the climber to ascend an unknown face.

This guidebook intends to document the exploratory--and in recent years creative--spirit of climbers and mountaineers who have used the rocks along the Potomac River for decades. It is a guide to some of the newer routes as well as a partial record of the people who first actively climbed the area and named many routes.

Newcomers may use this guide to introduce themselves to the extent of the rocks in the Carderock area. A companion guidebook, *A Climber's Guide to Great Falls* by James Eakin, describes the rocks in the Great Falls area, upriver from Carderock, and is available from the PATC and local climbing shops.

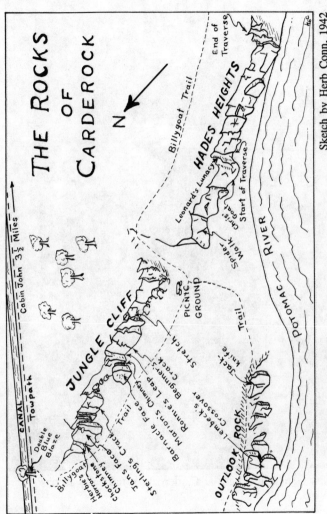

THE ROCKS OF CARDEROCK

N

Cabin John 3½ Miles

CANAL

Towpath

Double Blue Blaze

JUNGLE CLIFF

Billygoat Trail

Herbie's Horror

Chockstone Chimney

Jan's Crack

Sterling's Crack

Barnacle Face

Ronnie's Leap

Marion's Chimney

Beginner's Crack

Stretch

PICNIC GROUND

Spider Walk

Start of Traverse

Chris' Goat

Leonard's Lunacy

HADES HEIGHTS

End of Traverse

Trail

Crossover

Lembeck's Crossover

Jack-knife

OUTLOOK ROCK

POTOMAC RIVER

Sketch by Herb Conn, 1942

Gus Gambs lunching at Carderock in the early forties (Vos).

Introduction

Several cliffs are described in this guidebook, beginning
upriver on the Maryland side of the Potomac above the
main section of Carderock and continuing down the
riverbank to Camp Lewis. Boucher Rocks, opposite Camp
Lewis on the Virginia side are mentioned next. Scattered
cliffs along the Virginia shore are then listed as well as
cliffs on the nearby islands. Many of these areas, such as
Camp Lewis and Vaso Island, were popular in the 1940's,
yet today they tend to be overgrown with grape and
trumpet vine, honeysuckle, greenbriar, blackberry and
poison ivy. Nevertheless, the cliffs remain accessible and
publicizing these less frequented areas is to remind
climbers of other quality routes and crags, and to
document the climbing history at these areas. It is also to
bring attention to areas in need of conservation due to
erosion caused by the river, and to maintain public access.

Carderock has an erosion problem because of its proximity
to the river. Many climbs, such as those near Easy
Layback, have lost two feet of top soil at the bottom of
the route within a few decades. A large section of cliff,
containing the climb Sterling's Twin Cracks, is now
unreachable from below due to erosion. From records
forty years ago, it is evident that human use has increased
the rate of erosion by wearing away the vegetation which
holds the riverbank intact. Continued conservation of the
area by users is needed to preserve this unique climbing
playground.

An effort was made to record the first ascent of a climb
and to use the first name a climb was given. However, a
brief glance through the book shows that many climbs
were "first" named in the sixties. It is likely that routes
were put up before then. Unless it was possible to obtain

the original name, the name in use today is used and the first ascent attributed to the person who gave it that name.

The islands in the Potomac River south of Great Falls have long been used by climbers, though it is evident from their records that the island names have changed. For example, what is now referred to as Cleft Island appears as Cleft Island in maps before 1945, after which the U.S.G.S. Falls Church Quadrant Map cites it as Falls Island, and then Rocky Island by the 1956 edition. Because climbers have always called the island Cleft, it is assumed that the island became popular for climbing before 1945.

The same story is true for many other islands. Cupid's Bower is known as such, although the 1945 Falls Church Quadrant Map suddenly calls it Sherwin Island. The large island opposite Carderock was originally called Herzog. In 1945 it was renamed Vaso and the name Herzog given to a smaller island immediately upstream. Further upstream Himes Island becomes Offutt. Since climbing records refer to the old names, climbing on these islands must have been popular before the mid forties. It is interesting that climbers call the island adjacent to Vaso by the name Turkey Island. It was originally Scott Island and only became known as Turkey in the 1945 Falls Church Quadrant Map. Thus, climbing on this island must have been popular after 1945.

The current names of the islands will be used to follow the rules of the Board on Geographic Names which states that the currently printed name is valid unless it can be proven incorrect. Because the field notes of the surveyor for the Falls Church Quadrant Map for the 1945 edition are missing, it is not possible to determine why the names were changed.

History of Climbing in the Area

In the 1920's Gustave Gambs (1868-1958) first introduced
the sport of roped climbing to the area, and a new
dimension of Carderock began to be explored. Gus
Gambs, Donald Hubbard, and Paul Bradt were among the
climbers who began to spend time at Carderock. They
used heavy manila ropes, pounded pitons into cracks for
protection, and in addition to bottom to top routes, put up
traverses to get the maximum length routes on the
relatively short cliffs. Climbers tied into the rope with a
single loop around the waist and a bowline knot. Often
belays were from the top, though bottom belays became
more commonly used. Stiff mountain boots were worn, as
were boots with tricouni edge nails or simply inexpensive
sneakers.

During the war years, Carderock was approached by trolley
from Georgetown to Cabin John, and then a 4 mile walk
along the Canal to the cliffs. It was a much shorter walk
to Lewis Rocks, now known as Camp Lewis. During the
gas rationing years of the war, when Great Falls was
visited less often, Carderock was used even more
frequently. This was especially the case beginning in
November 1943 when the last Saturday half holiday for
government workers was suspended. Between 1931-1943,
government employees had to work half of Saturday,
leaving only Sunday free for climbing. Some areas
upriver, such as Cupid's Bower, were on restricted areas
and opened to climbers again only after August 1945, a
few days after gas rationing days ended. Carderock
remained popular in these years, even after other areas
became accessible again. By 1946 the Capitol Transit Bus
System began running much closer to Carderock, although
it was rarely used.

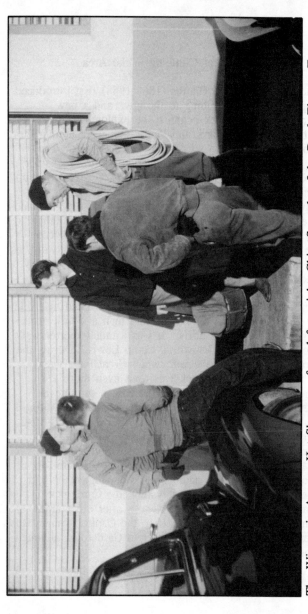

The Wisconsin Avenue Hot Shoppes: from left to right, Chirs Scoredos, John Reed, Eleanor Tatge, Earl Mosburg, and Don Hubbard (Wexler).

Climbing in the 1940's was an era of scouting, climbing, cave exploring, equipment testing and designing. New equipment was often introduced, as the war years had recruited many of the regular weekend climbers, and they came back with the latest version of carabiners, ropes and shoes.

The rocks served for more than just recreation during the war years. Often joining the locals Herb and Jan Conn, and others, was a group from the Army Quartermasters Corps: Bestor Robinson, Richard Leonard and Ernar Nielson from California; and Bob Bates and Bill House from New England. These men were developing climbing and mountaineering equipment for the Army. Dick Leonard is reported to have compared the U.S. and the British climbing shoes by wearing one on each foot. As he unexpectedly came off of a climb, he cursed the British boot. Also at Carderock, at the request of the Quartermasters Corps, the Bureau of Standards made what was probably one of the first tests of the holding power of pitons. Many of the people who climbed at this time are familar to us through the names of routes. The Conns are remembered in Herbie's Horror and Jan's Face at Carderock, Conn's East and West at Seneca and Conncourse on Cannon Cliff, New Hampshire. Jan is from Bethesda, Maryland, and Herb from Geneva, New York. They had scrambled as kids together near summer homes in New Hampshire's White Mountains. Herb came to the Washington, D.C. area in 1942. After founding *Up Rope* in November 1944 and acting as editors until October 1945, the Conns moved to Boulder, and eventually to Custer, South Dakota, where they still reside.

The record of the achievements and attempts of climbers can be found in the newsletter *Up Rope*, begun in 1944 by Herb and Jan Conn. *Up Rope* was the newsletter of a

John Reed ready for a belay test with Oscar, Sam Brown
on platform above (Wexler 1951).

group called The Washington Rock Climbers and was
intended to increase the activity of climbers by informing
them of meetings, new places to climb, and other people
interested in climbing. By 1950, the Washington Rock
Climbers joined the Potomac Appalachian Trail Club
(PATC) as the Mountaineering Committee. The newsletter
still continues under the PATC Mountaineering Section.

Lists of Qualifying Climbs were made by the club which
needed to be completed before a newcomer could join the
Washington Rock Climbers. The list included climbs at
Carderock, Camp Lewis, Herzog and Echo Cliffs along the
Potomac, as well as Sugarloaf Mountain, Maryland; Bull
Run Mountain, Virginia, and Seneca Rocks, West Virginia.

During the war years, there were five climbers who
faithfully met at the Wisconsin Avenue Hot Shoppes: Herb
and Jan Conn, Donald Hubbard, Eleanor Tatge, and Arnold
Wexler, and the Conn's dogs Piton and Carabiner (Pete
and Beaner). Others frequently joined, such as Paul Bradt,
Sterling Hendricks, Arthur Lembeck, and Chris Scoredos.
Ice skating or swimming in the river were supplements to
a day of putting up a new traverse. There was also
Eleanor Tatge's Sink Stopper, a rubber Army life raft
which was used to ferry climbers across to Vaso Island,
then called Herzog.

The Hot Shoppes remained the meeting place for many
years for members of the Washington Rock Climbers. In a
note to climbers in a 1960 *Up Rope*, there was a serious
plea that climbers not call the Hot Shoppes and ask where
the trip was going. Instead, any latecomer could find a
note behind a drain pipe outside of the restaurant. After
climbing, people usually gathered at someone's house for
dinner. This tradition changed over the years and people
gathered at Tuohey's in Cabin John. Around five o'clock
on a summer evening it was common to hear the cry

"Tuohey Time." After that establishment burned down, people went for sandwiches at Roys in Gaithersburg or for chile at Trav's in Glen Echo.

In addition to climbing trips, the group conducted other activites to enhance the climbers skill. Dynamic belaying, a technique pioneered by Arnold Wexler and Richard Leonard, needed practice. In 1946 a belay practice system was rigged from a large sycamore near the walkdown separating Jungle Cliffs from Hades Heights. A 150 pound log called Oscar simulated the falling leader. Practice belays were first done from the ground. For more realism a belay platform was built high up in the tree and Oscar was hauled up by a number of climbers pulling on a rope.

By 1954 Oscar II was constructed. A steel drum filled with cement, weighing 145 pounds, required more technology. "Operation Uplift," or "Operation Crash," as it became known, required expansion bolts, a portable gas engine, a windlass and the faithful Mount Sycamore. A film of Oscar II was made which records the belaying techniques and styles of the time. The sycamore no longer stands.

By the 1950's, a group of active climbers joined the group at Carderock. These included John Christian, Andy Kaufman and in the early sixties Jim Shipley. The most noticeable top rope feat was the successfull ascent of the Jam Box by Tony Soler. Although perhaps a few more holds were available then, rated at 5.10 this was clearly a remarkable accomplishment for the time.

The number of active climbers continued to grow in the 1960's. Climbers of the era included Charlie Rollins, Matt Hale, Joe Faint, Bob Norris, and Charlie Fowler. Fowler is known for his climbing at Yosemite; and Faint is

known to local climbers for Faint's Roof (5.9) at
Annapolis Rock. As climbing techniques rapidly advanced,
a new sport to rock climbing was developed. John
Stannard began putting up new boulder problems, very
hard problems such as those found at Stannards Playground
on the Outlook Rocks.

In December 1964 the parkway between the Beltway and
MacArthur Boulevard was opened. Access to the cliffs
was made easier in 1965 when the National Park Service
opened the Carderock Recreation Area with several parking
lots. There were also picnic areas, including one close to
Jungle Cliffs. The PATC Mountaineering Section
expressed concern to the National Park Service of the
potential hazards of a picnic area above the cliffs. The
National Park Service removed the picnic area, leaving the
last parking lot for climbers and towpath users.

In the sixties and seventies hard routes were put up, and
climbers developed many "new" climbs sometimes only
inches from previous climbs. For many who began
coming to the rocks, climbing became a part of life around
which to organize the rest of life, perhaps more so than in
the past. Rock climbing also developed into a technical
sport. There was a transition from the stiff "Spiders" to
shoes called R.D.'s, and the latter led to the smearing
E.B.'s. In August 1967 Tom Evans returned from a trip
to Yosemite with chalk.

In the 1970's, the most difficult top rope climb finally
ascended was Silverspot, by Mike Banks. The number of
boulder problems continued to grow, as did the climbers.
These included, among others, Mel Banks, John Bercaw,
Greg Collins, Howard Doyle, Greg Hand, Buddy Guthrie,
John Stannard, Lotus Steele, and Leith Wain. Local
residents John Gregory and Carderock Jeff were climbing
on the rocks as well.

By 1974 the popularity of Carderock was evident in the trampled vegetation and bare soil. John Stannard and Chuck Sproull, with help from other climbers, made steps by Elsie's Other Edgeface and placed logs to define the trail.

In 1981 an informal Carderock Erosion Study was made, leading quickly to a Carderock Conservation Project. Janet Young, Mike Chaney and local climbers combined forces with the National Park Service to perform needed erosion control and trail work. A railroad tie retaining wall was placed along the riverbank near Cripple's to reclaim the pathway which provides access to many climbs. Fifty-five railroad ties were obtained from the B & O Railroad, courtesy of Josh Letman, a local climber, and were stripped of hardware and brought to the cliffs by several local climbers. In addition, willow shrubs were planted.

In July 1982 a stepping stone walkway from the parking lot to the cliffs was built and by September 1982 a 100 ft boardwalk over this marshy area was constructed by John Christian and others with donations of timber from F. Bowie Smith & Son, Inc. and of nails from the National Park Service.

Over the years these efforts have withstood foot traffic and floods, but conservation of the area is an ongoing concern for all recreational users at Carderock. In July 1987 the PATC Mountaineering Section and John Gregory met with the National Park Service to renew renovation efforts to repair the retaining walls and trails. These efforts finally culminated in a revised work plan and in May 1988 the conservation work was begun again. At the time of this guide's writing, work continues on the Carderock Conservation Project.

In 1980 John Gregory's guidebook to Carderock appeared, recording the many climbs that had been done in the area. The eighties continue with hard core climbers, all of whom continue to use Carderock as a place to practice for taller cliffs.

Though the rocks get older and smoother and generations of climbers come and go, there remains a valued resource which has changed the lives of many as they challenge themselves to climbing the rocks.

Ann Remington on Lembeck's Crossover (Reed 1952)

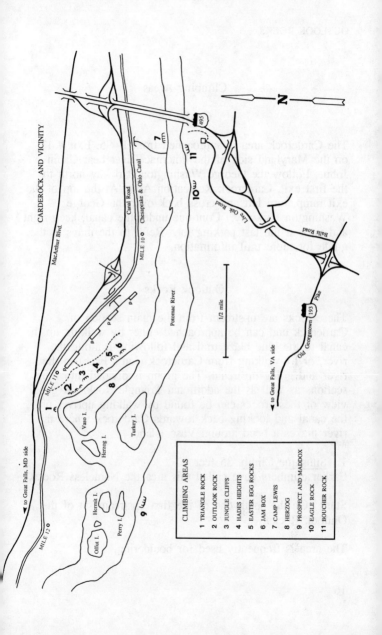

CARDEROCK AND VICINITY

N

to Great Falls, MD side

MILE 12 ○

MILE 11 ○

MILE 10 ○

MILE 11 ○

Offut I.

Hermit I.

Perry I.

Vaso I.

Herzog I.

Turkey I.

Potomac River

MacArthur Blvd.

Canal Road

Chesapeake & Ohio Canal

Live Oak Road

495

Balls Road

Old Georgetown Pike

193

to Great Falls, VA via

1/2 mile

1
2
3
4
5
6
8
9

7

10

11

CLIMBING AREAS

1 TRIANGLE ROCK
2 OUTLOOK ROCK
3 JUNGLE CLIFFS
4 HADES HEIGHTS
5 EASTER EGG ROCKS
6 JAM BOX
7 CAMP LEWIS
8 HERZOG
9 PROSPECT AND MADDOX
10 EAGLE ROCK
11 BOUCHER ROCK

Climbing Areas

Carderock

The Carderock area is approached from I-495, Exit # 13, on the Maryland side of the Potomac River near Cabin John. Follow the George Washington Parkway north to the first exit, Carderock Recreation Area. At the top of the exit ramp, turn left and cross back over the George Washington Parkway. Continue under the canal, keep right and park at the last parking lot. Refer to the maps in the guide for more trail information.

Outlook Rocks

These rocks are upstream from the main section of Carderock and can be approached either by walking up the canal to the blue blaze trail and following it along the river, or by walking from Carderock (Jan's Face) to the river and going upstream. The group is divided into four sections as well as the additional Triangle Rock. A good view of these rocks can be found by walking upriver on the canal and looking back towards Carderock where the river makes a bend around Vaso Island.

1. <u>Sunshine Climb</u>, 35 feet
Earlier climbers have called this area the Nameless Rocks.

Start: On the south end of the first upstream set of the Outlook Rocks.

The area is frequently used for bouldering.

16

1. Nameless

OUTLOOK ROCKS

①

2. Lembeck's Crossover, 5.3, 35 feet
This traverse was first climbed by Arthur Lembeck in 1940
with Paul Bradt as second, and has been known as
Arthur's Crossover or Arthur's Traverse. Arthur Lembeck
began climbing in the 1930's at Carderock. He had a
career in the Navy and when his tour of duty allowed him
to be in the Washington D.C. area, he climbed at
Carderock.

Start: On the second set of rocks, on a shelf under a
small overhang.

The traverse diagonals upwards and downstream along a
crack. The route can be continued by climbing up the
face once the traverse has been completed and climbing
the overhang on the left.

3. The Nose That Goes, 5.8, 35 feet
Start: Same as Lembeck's Crossover.

Follow the right edge, climb over the overhang and
continue straight up. If the left edge is not used except
for the first step, the route is 5.10.

Another variation of Lembeck's Crossover starts under the
left side of the overhang below a small vertical crack.
The hairline crack is followed until it is possible to mantle.
Proceed up and right past the next left facing edge. The
overhang can also be climbed slightly to the left of the
middle, pulling up on a finger tip undercling (The Nose
That Blows, 5.10).

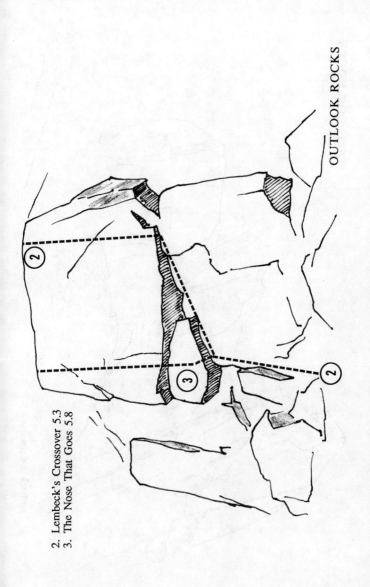

2. Lembeck's Crossover 5.3
3. The Nose That Goes 5.8

OUTLOOK ROCKS

OUTLOOK ROCKS

2. Lembeck's Crossover 5.3

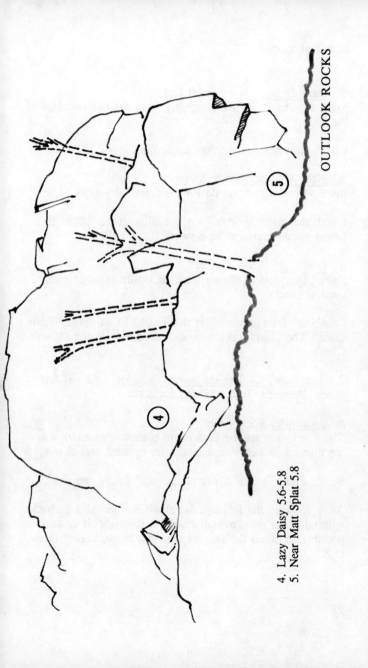

OUTLOOK ROCKS

4. Lazy Daisy 5.6-5.8
5. Near Matt Splat 5.8

4. <u>Lazy Daisy</u>, 5.6 - 5.8, 30 feet
Start: On the set of rocks upriver from the main section of
the cliff.

Climb anywhere on the low angle face.

5. <u>Near Matt Splat</u>, 5.8, 25 feet
Start: Near waterlevel downriver from Lazy Daisy face.

Climb the layback corner. A variation to the left in the
finger corner can also be done (5.10).

6. <u>Guillotine</u>, 5.9+, 30 feet
Start: Four feet upstream from Jackknife between two
vertical cracks.

Climb the face between the two cracks to an upside down
flake. The climb has also been called the Upside Down
Climb.

7. <u>The Tomb Of The Unknown Shoulder</u>, 5.12, 30 feet
Start: Between Guillotine and Jackknife.

8. <u>Jackknife</u>, 5.5, 30 feet
The climb was named because of someone's remark that
the climber looked like a jackknife, opening and closing.

Start: Small inside corner on the wall facing the river.

After working the feet up, the climb is done as a layback
without using the diagonal crack on the right. It is also
possible to climb the face to the right of the corner crack
(5.8 - 5.9).

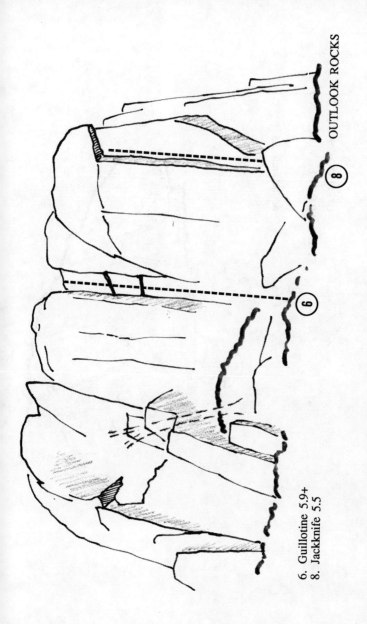

OUTLOOK ROCKS

6. Guillotine 5.9+
8. Jackknife 5.5

OUTLOOK ROCKS -
STANNARDS PLAYGROUND

8. Jackknife 5.5

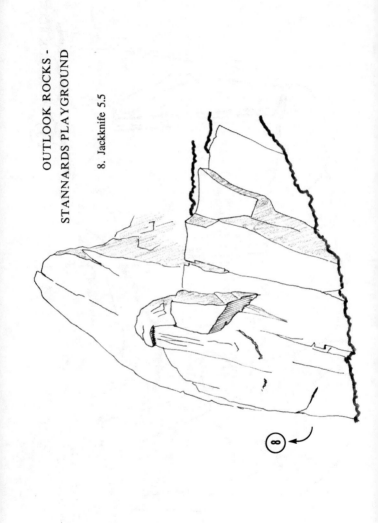

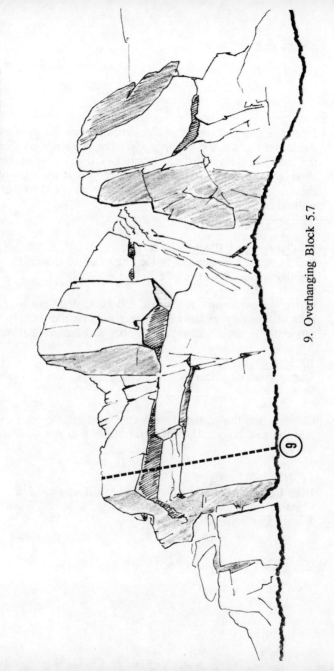

JUNGLE CLIFFS

9. Overhanging Block 5.7

Jungle Cliffs

From the end parking lot at Carderock, follow the path by the latrines to the top of the cliffs. The cliffs upriver from the walkdown are called the Jungle Cliffs, referring to the abundant vegetation that at one time existed at the base of these cliffs. Routes are listed from upstream (left) to the walkdown.

9. <u>Overhanging Block</u>, 5.7, 20 feet
Start: On the first boulder at the beginning of the cliff, approximately 50 feet left of Jan's Face.

Climb the overhang. A traverse can be started here which goes all the way to Jan's Face: stay only on the rock, especially in the Chockstone Chimney and around the tree.

10. <u>Jam Crack</u>, 5.2, 25 feet
Start: On an easy face below a crack 25 feet left of Jan's Face.

Climb to the top of the sloping face, step off the edge and into the jam crack. Use holds on the face to reach out to the top.

11. <u>Herbie's Horror</u>, 5.9, 25 feet
Herb Conn first climbed this in 1942, and inspired Jan Conn to write the following verse, to the tune of "When Johnny Comes Marchin' Home."

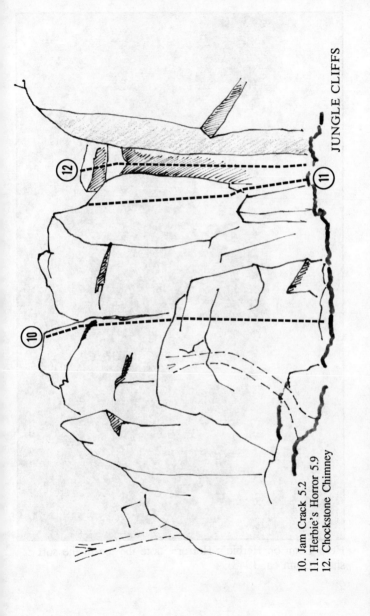

JUNGLE CLIFFS

10. Jam Crack 5.2
11. Herbie's Horror 5.9
12. Chockstone Chimney

Herb Conn on Herbie's Horror: note the toe in the soft shoe (Conn ca. 1943).

Arnold Wexler on Herbie's Horror (Wexler).

29

When your foot begins a slippin' and you think
you're gonna fall,
And what you're hangin' onto isn't any good at all,
And there's nothing quite within your reach that's
half as good to use,
That's the time you get those "Herbie's Horror"
Blues.
Oh, the "Herbie's Horror" Blues make you feel so
low,
And you wonder what it is that makes you fall off
so,
And you tear your hair in deep despair and blame it
on your shoes-
But we all know it's the "Herbie's Horror" Blues.

(Author Jan Conn wrote the following note about the
climb: "Herbie's Horror: The name of a climb at
Carderock which never should have been done.
Unfortunately it was successfully ascended three times.
Thereafter it was banned as being injurious to the morale
and mental stability of the rock climber.").

Start: Left face of a chimney upstream from Jan's Face.

The standard climb ascends the wall just left of center.
The climb can be made more difficult by further to the
right (5.11).

12. <u>Chockstone Chimney</u>, 5.3, 35 feet
Start: At the base of the large chimney left of Jan's Face.

Tradition dictates that the climb be done using the chimney
technique, and not by climbing the easy route up the
corner.

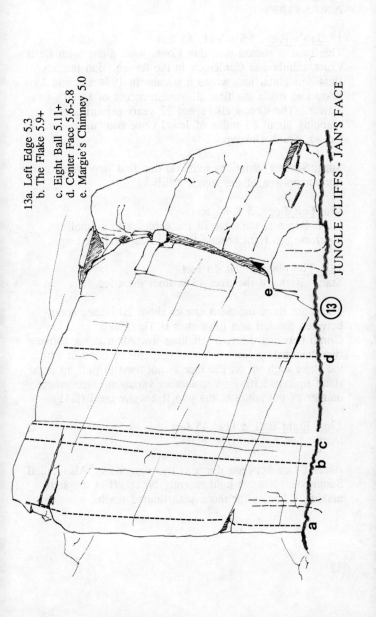

13a. Left Edge 5.3
  b. The Flake 5.9+
  c. Eight Ball 5.11+
  d. Center Face 5.6-5.8
  e. Margie's Chimney 5.0

⑬ JUNGLE CLIFFS - JAN'S FACE

13. <u>Jan's Face</u>, 5.6 - 5.11, 45 feet
This face is named after Jan Conn, who, along with Herb
Conn, climbed at Carderock in the forties. Jan teaches
flute and guitar and writes musicals. In 1954 she and Jane
Showacre made the first all-woman ascent of Devil's
Tower. The Conns also spent 22 years exploring and
mapping about 65 miles of Jewel Cave near their home in
Custer, South Dakota.

Start: Several variations exist on this first large face on the
upriver portion of the Jungle Cliffs.

13a. <u>Left Edge</u>, 5.3, 45 feet
Start: Begin at the edge of the chimney to a small
overhang, go right around the overhang and then up.

13b. <u>The Flake</u>, 5.9+, 45 feet
Start: Right of the tree, 15 ft from the edge.

There are three incipient cracks about 20 inches apart,
between the left and the center is The Flake.
Climb between the two left lines towards a flake, above
two diagonaling lines. A variation can be done in which
the flake high up on the face is not used to pull up or to
stand up on (5.10+). Yet another variation exists where
neither of the holds in the two flakes are used (5.11).

13c. <u>Eight Ball</u>, 5.11+, 45 feet
Start: Just right of The Flake.

Ascend face between the next two diagonals. Also called
Stannards. Note: a hold recently broke off at the start,
making it harder for those with limited reach.

13d. <u>Center Face</u>, 5.6 - 5.8, 45 feet
Start: Anywhere between Eight Ball and Margie's
Chimney.

A variety of classic face climbs can be found on this wall.

13e. <u>Margie's Chimney</u>, 5.0, 45 feet
This was also known as Margie's Cave in the 1940's.

Start: Base of a wide crack in Jan's Face.

Follow chimney to top.

14. <u>Elsie's Other</u>, 5.7, 45 feet
In the 1940's this part of the cliff was called Stolen
Handhold.

Start: Slanting grooved face around the right corner of
Jan's Face.

Balance up the groove in the center, which is easier on the
right. A variation can be done by staying left in the
groove (5.9).

15. <u>Three Chimney Climb</u>
Although rarely climbed today, this was a favorite climb in
the 1940's and 1950's and was referred to as the Grunt
and Groan Chimney. One went up the left chimney, down
the center one and up the right one. The left chimney has
since been given the name Thin Man's. The climb ended
in the route now called The Rack.

Start: At the base of the first chimney around the right
corner of Jan's Face.

33

16. <u>The Dream</u>, 5.11, 40 feet
Greg Hand had a dream how to do this climb, which he
tried the next day and succeeded in the first ascent.

Start: Same as Three Chimney Climb.

Climb up under the large overhanging block, hand traverse
right along the lip of the overhang to the center. Pull the
overhang with a foot smear in the small notch.

16a. <u>The Dream Direct</u>, 5.11+, 40 feet
Start: Directly below the center of the overhang described
in The Dream.

Approach the center of the overhang, using a knee lock to
reach the crucial hand hold at the lip. Pull the overhang
at the small notch. The climb starts on The Wet Dream
and finishes on The Dream. F.A. by Greg Hand.

16b. <u>Wet Dream</u>, 5.12-, 40 feet
Start: Same as The Dream Direct.

Use a right heel hook above the notch, then bring hands
up high on the face. F.A. by Hunt Prothro, who began
climbing at Carderock in 1971 and makes a living as an
artist.

16c. <u>Twitch</u>, 5.12, 40 feet
Start: Same as The Dream.

Traverse to the edge with the hands, using the far right
face for the feet. Hook feet around flake and layback.
F.A. by Charlie Rollins on the same day that Prothro did
the Wet Dream, which Rollins was not able to do. Rollins
is a physician and currently lives in Boulder, Colorado.

17. <u>Death Nerve</u>, 5.10-, 40 feet
Start: Same as for Vulgarian Wedge.

Climb the right side of the Dream block using a flake to a long reach. A lunge move.

18. <u>Vulgarian Wedge</u>, 5.9+, 40 feet
Start: From a block right of The Dream roof.

Climb up the wedge shaped flake. If only the outside face of the wedge is used, the route is 5.11.

19. <u>Fat Man's Fantasy</u>, 5.6, 40 feet
Start: Same as Vulgarian Wedge.

Chimney up the rock, between the Vulgarian Wedge and The Rack on the right.

20. <u>The Rack</u>, 5.7, 40 feet
Start: At the wall between Sterling's Crack and a small left facing corner 15 feet left of Sterling's Crack.

Climb to top of block, up face and over the bulge. Finish on the easier face.

21. <u>The Rack Direct</u>, 5.11-, 40 feet
First climbed in 1974 by Chips Janger, who called it The Rack Arete. Several climbers were working on the climb when Janger arrived after not climbing for years and did it onsight.

Start: At the bottom of the outside corner to the left of Sterling's Crack.

JUNGLE CLIFFS

Using perhaps an undercling (or perhaps something else), move up to the right edge and quartz nubbins on the left face; then work the feet high enough to reach better handholds. Pull the overhang. Keeping balance, continue up the arete to the top.

22. Sterling's Crack, 5.7, 40 feet
Sterling Hendricks (1902-1981) was an excellent rock climber, mountaineer, and scientist. He started climbing in the 1920's. At Carderock this climb is named after him as well as Sterling's Twin Cracks. There are also the climbs Sterling's Little Quartz Slab and Sterling's Corner at Bull Run, Virginia. He put up at least fifty first ascents, with many more second ascents, of remote peaks in British Columbia and Alaska. In 1942 the Army Quartermaster arranged an expedition to Mt. McKinley and invited Hendricks along to assist in equipment evaluation for the first U.S. mountaineering troops. Erner Nielson, Bestor Robinson and Bob Bates were also along. It was at this time that Bates gave Hendricks his nickname Strawberry, for his reddish blond hair and ruddy complexion. Hendricks was a member of the National Academy

---

Routes for map on page 32

14. Elsie's Other 5.7
16. The Dream 5.11
17. Death Nerve 5.10-
18. Vulgarian Wedge 5.9+
20. The Rack 5.7
21. The Rack Direct 5.11-
22. Sterling's Crack 5.7
23. Evan's Bolt Ladder
24. Elsie's 5.5 - 5.7

---

of Science, and was chief scientist at the Department of Agriculture. He was a generalist, competent in many fields of science, and was a pioneer in the discovery of phytochrome.

Start: At the foot of a crack in a downstream facing corner, about 25 feet from the right edge of Jan's Face.

Using a layback with the hands in the well worn crack, climb to the top. Although originally part of the climb, the horn at the top is not used with either the feet or the hands. A variation named Left Face goes up the left face to the horn (5.9+).

23. Evan's Bolt Ladder, A1 or 5.12, 40 feet
In the winter of 1969 Tom Evans placed the Bolt Ladder on a lead. After talking with climbers, this site was chosen because it was a face unlikely to be climbed free, since the flakes on it are sloping downward. Placing the bolts, hauling rigs, and setting up belays were in preparation for Big Wall climbing. Tom Evans climbed at Carderock from 1965-71.

Evans was not the first to place bolts on this face. In April 1954 Andy Kauffman also put in bolts, also to practice for climbs out West. Neither man would place these bolts today at Carderock, though they admit that at the time, it was an acceptable practice.

Aid Start: Below the face right of Sterling's Crack. According to Tom Evans, these bolts went in easily, are old, and should not be trusted.

Free Start: The face just right of Sterling's Crack has been climbed (5.12).

24. <u>Elsie's</u>, 5.5 - 5.7, 40 feet
This climb was originally called Elsie's Edgeface, and
although some say Elsie's identity is unknown, others say
she is Elsie of Borden Milk Product fame. F.A. Chris
Scoredos, 1944.

Start: On the flakes on the sloping wall before the cliff
recesses, right of Sterling's Crack.

Follow the grooves up the cliff. The easiest groove is on
the right side of the face and each groove is harder as you
move to the left. Half way up the face, The Chimney
Variation (5.8) moves left to a shallow groove and then
chimneys up this groove.

24a. <u>Elsie's Nose</u>, 5.10, 40 feet
Start: On the flakes on the left side of Elsie's.

Begin climbing face as a layback, work feet up, grab small
knob with left hand and continue up and left. Strenuous,
especially if the bottom moves have not been worked out.

24b. <u>The Nose Direct</u>, 5.11, 40 feet
Start: Just left of Elsie's Nose.

Layback through the overhang to the small knob, then
follow the left slanting diagonal crack and face up the
arete.

24c. <u>The Nose Direct Direct</u>, 5.11+, 40 feet
Start: Below overhang

Climb directly over the overhang left of the Nose Direct
and stay left of left slanting crack. Stays completely left of
crack. Think toe hook.

A third class descent route is possible in the chimney behind the tree, but is usually dirty.

25. <u>Upper Wall Crack</u>, 5.1, 20 feet
Start: The face above and right of Elsie's and above Barnacle Face.

Often soloed, this can be done as a face climb or a layback. There are also face climbs to the right of the crack (5.8, 5.10).

26. <u>Upper Wall Jam Crack</u>, 5.0, 15 feet
Start: Crack to the right of Upper Wall Crack.

Often used as an easy solo route to get up and down this area of the cliff.

27. <u>The X</u>, 5.7, 30 feet
Start: On Barnacle Face, below the X formed by the inverted "V" shaped overhang and the incipient cracks.

Climb up to and beyond the cracks which form The X without using the holds in or on the cracks.

28. <u>Barnacle Face</u>, 5.3, 30 feet
Start: The large block leaning against the cliffs left of Beginner's Crack.

This face is used for bouldering and also contains the two climbs, The X and Wexler's Worst and Stretch.

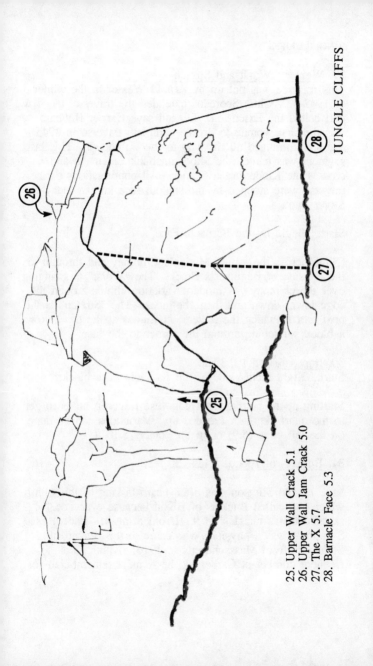

JUNGLE CLIFFS

25. Upper Wall Crack 5.1
26. Upper Wall Jam Crack 5.0
27. The X 5.7
28. Barnacle Face 5.3

29. Wexler's Worst and Stretch
This traverse was put up by Arnold Wexler in the winter of 1942-43. Chris Scoredos extended the traverse, the new part called the Extension. Legend says Harriet Hubbard was the first woman to do the complete traverse in 1945 and she continued all the way to the walkdown. This last segment was named the Skookumchuck Extension and crosses the Kindergarten Corner. All continuations of the traverse were stopped by the smooth face known today as Silver Spot.

Start: Begin by the Barnacle Face.

Climb across the top of Marian's Chimney and through to the far side of Beginner's Crack. The "Worst" is swinging over the chimney. A modern variation climbs around the edge lower down and then continues. The "Stretch" is the next part in which the traverse continues at the top below a block, stretching around the corner to the face.

30. Impossible, 5.10, 30 feet
Start: Right facing side of the Barnacle Face block.

Starting at the bottom right edge use fingertip holds to get to the quartz knobs. Proceed up. Variations can be done on the left edge (5.9) or in the center (5.10+).

31. Buckets of Blood, 5.11+, 30 feet

Mrs. Harold Stimson was often heard talking of this climb which she called Buckets of Blood because everyone skinned their knuckles on it. Harold Stimson --known as Stimmie-- was a physicist who came to the Bureau of Standards from Massachusetts in 1916. Although a frequent climber at Carderock, he is most remembered for

a camp he had at Cupid's Bower. "Stimmie's College of
Climbing Knowledge" refers to the academic climbs on the
island which he first scouted and brought to the attention
of climbers.

Start: On the back side of Impossible.
Crank up, slap palm around the left edge, use heel hook,
and move up. At the top one moves left around the
corner. A hard variation can be done by staying on the
back side and not using the edge. One of the flake holds
broke off recently, making this route just a little harder.

32. <u>Marian's Chimney</u>, 5.4, 30 feet
This route is rarely done today, and is named for Marian
Grove Churchill who frequented the area in the 1930's and
40's before moving to Mexico.

Start: Base of a wide chimney formed by the left side of
the Barnacle Face.

33. <u>Swayback Layback</u>, 5.8, 40 feet
Start: At rib 15 feet left of Ronnie's Leap and 6 feet
right of Marian's Chimney.

Layback and face climb, using slippery holds, toward the
crack. Continue right and follow crack to the top. Care
must be taken when rigging this climb, as the anchor rope
tends to pinch in a vicious crack.

34. <u>Swollen Head</u>, 5.10-, 40 feet
This climb is named in part because of the bulging rock,
and in part because of Greg Hand's inflated ego as John
Stannard couldn't do it right after Hand made the first
ascent. Greg Hand is known for his humor and fitness.

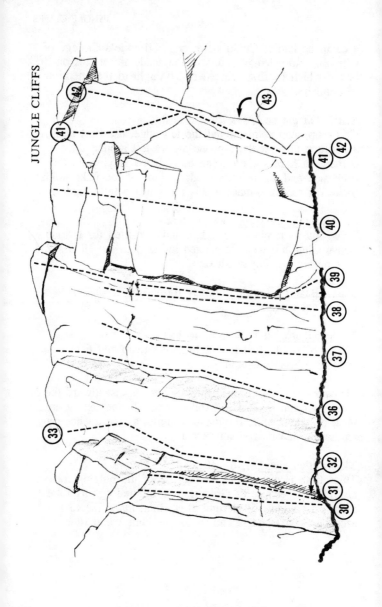

JUNGLE CLIFFS

Start: At a rib, 8 feet left of Ronnie's Leap, between Swayback Layback and Shipley's.

Follow the rib. Use a combination of knobs as well as small right and left laybacks.

35. <u>Shipley's</u>, 5.9, 40 feet
Start: Left of Ronnie's Leap 4 feet, to the right of Swayback Layback.

Climb face between rib and Ronnie's Leap by balancing up to prominant hold on the face and continuing straight on the face. If the great pinch hold is not used, the climb is more difficult (5.11-). First climbed by Baltimore artist Jim Shipley, known for Triple S at Seneca.

36. <u>Ronnie's Leap</u>, 5.7, 40 feet
The dog Ronnie belonged to a neighbor of Jan Conn's. Stories differ, but apparently Ronnie saw a rabbit or squirrel below, charged over the cliff, and landed at the base, unhurt but surprised.

Start: At small 2 foot wide face to the right of the crack 10 feet left of Beginner's Face.

Ascend face without using holds in the crack. The crux is at the bottom. Try not to use the big holds to the right.

Beginner's Crack (Wexler)

46

37. <u>The Bump</u>, 5.8, 40 feet
Start: On the muddy face 10 feet left of Beginner's Crack.

Climb straight up through the bump.

38. <u>The Diamond</u>, 5.8, 40 feet
Start: At face between Beginner's Crack and the left
flake.

Climb up using only the face to surmount the diamond.
Once above it, continue left towards the top.

39. <u>Beginner's Crack</u>, 5.3, 40 feet
Start: In an amphitheater 100 feet upstream from the
walkdown at the prominent crack 40 feet to the right of
Barnacle Face.

The climb can be done with a combination of techniques,
either jamming, using a layback, or using face holds to
ascend the two small overhangs. The holds are worn and
the start is hard.

40. <u>Beginner's Face</u>, 5.4, 40 feet
Start: The face right of Beginner's Crack.

The climb is easier if started on the left and more difficult
if begun in the center. This face was known as Sterling's
Test in the 1940's and 50's.

41. <u>Meenehan's Staircase</u>, 5.5, 30 feet
This was first climbed by John Meenehan, a professional
photographer, who climbed in the 40's at Carderock and
still lives in the area. He is a member of the National
Speleological Society and was part of a group
whichmapped Schoolhouse Cave in Seneca, W.V. Paul

Bradt invited the group, including Jack Wilson, Bill Schlecht, Tom Culverwell and others, to learn the skills of mountaineering and to practice rock climbing before extensively mapping Schoolhouse Cave.

Start: Left end of Beginner's Face at the edge of the rock.

Climb the face diagonaling left, ending between the two blocks.

42. <u>Meenehan's Edge</u>, 5.8, 30 feet
Start: Same as Meenehan's Staircase.

Today the climb is called Meenehan's and is done as a right layback with the feet close to the edge. Although it may seem easier to use left handholds on the face about 8 inches from the edge, these are off route and often lead to an off balance position. This climb can be done one handed. A 5.10 finish requires a layback on the upper block.

43. <u>The Sloth</u>, 5.11, 25 feet
Start: Base of overhanging rock behind Meenehan's.

Assume a sloth position and climb the back side of Meenehan's Edge using feet on the edge as well as heel and toe hooks to get up while hands layback and pinch. The swing will land one on the opposite rock face, but rarely without warning.

A climb called The Shinny was done in the fifties in this corner. Climb up to the ax blade and stand on its sloping ledge. The crux of the climb then is to get left onto the face. Continue up over the block.

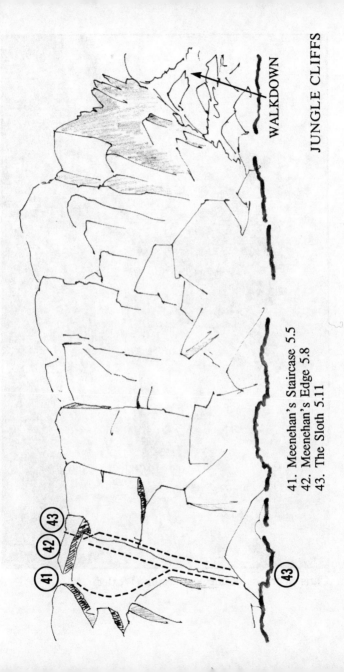

WALKDOWN

JUNGLE CLIFFS

41. Meenehan's Staircase 5.5
42. Meenehan's Edge 5.8
43. The Sloth 5.11

Chris Scoredos on the Spiderwalk (Wexler)

Hades Heights

These are the cliffs downstream from the Jungle Cliffs, separated by the main walkdown.

44. <u>Kindergarten</u>, 5.0, 25 feet
Start: Downstream face adjacent to the walkdown.

Good beginner's climb although the trail is close.

45. <u>The Nose</u>, 5.3, 30 feet
Start: The rounded arete between Kindergarten and Spiderwalk.

Follow the face to the top.

46. <u>Spider Walk</u>, 5.7, 30 feet
Sometimes referred to as Spider Crack, this was first climbed by Herb Conn in 1943.

Start: Left diagonal crack 20 feet downstream from the walkdown.

Layback to the top. The climb can also be done as a jam or using face holds.

47. <u>Silver Spot</u>, 5.10, 30 feet
The first ascent was in 1962 by Mike Banks, a British Marine stationed at Quantico who has climbed in the Himalayas.

This climb is a trifle hard for its grade, but reflects a time honored Carderock tradition of the early eighties.

51

Start: Begin 6 feet right of Spider Walk, to the right of a crescent vertical groove.

Climb up and onto the crescent groove; move up and slightly left, then continue on the thin face to the top.

48. Biceps, 5.9, 30 feet
This was formerly called The Cave Climb and was done by Herb Conn and Sterling Hendricks in 1945.

Start: Below an open book forming an overhang, 50 feet downstream of the walkdown.

Climb the overhang in the middle. Several climbs have been named as variations.

a. Thumbthing, 5.11-, 30 feet
Start: Same as Biceps.

Climb the left side of the overhang of Biceps laybacking the left edge of the block. Pull overhang.

b. Thumbthing Else, 5.11-, 30 feet
Start: Same as Biceps.

Step up below the lip of the overhang. Step right, and use an undercling to pull the overhang and reach the crack.

c. Right Wall, 5.10+, 30 feet
Start: Lower right edge of the Biceps overhang.

Move right, up face, using laybacks and a mantle finish.

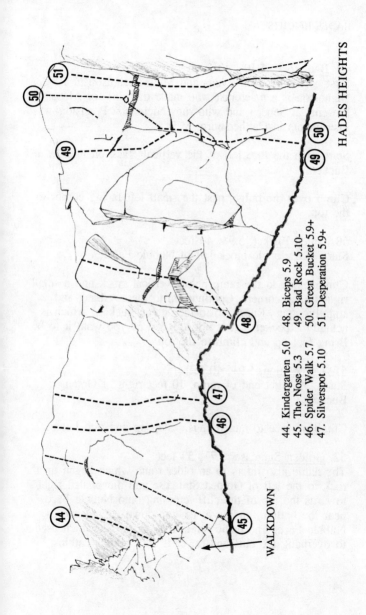

HADES HEIGHTS

WALKDOWN

44. Kindergarten 5.0
45. The Nose 5.3
46. Spider Walk 5.7
47. Silverspot 5.10

48. Biceps 5.9
49. Bad Rock 5.10-
50. Green Bucket 5.9+
51. Desperation 5.9+

49. <u>Bad Rock</u>, 5.10-, 40 feet
First ascent by Tom Evans and Mike Nicholson in 1968.
Nicholson is a machinist who made the pins for Alcoa
Presents at Seneca and who runs Nicholson Precision
Instruments in Gaithersburg, M.D.

Start: On the face left of the vertical crack on the Green
Bucket.

Climb over the bulge, past the small left facing corner to
the top.

50. <u>Green Bucket</u>, 5.9+, 40 feet
Start: Low angle block left of Nubble Face.

Climb block to the ramp below vertical crack and a small
right facing corner. Continue up to the overhang and
slightly right. Reach up to the "green bucket," which is
actually a pocket that is not as good as you want it to be.
Bring feet up and climb to the top.

51. <u>Desperation</u>, 5.9+, 40 feet
Start: At right end of ramp, 10 feet right of Green
Bucket.

Climb up face to underclings. Step up and pull bulge.

52. <u>Golden Staircase</u>, 5.7+, 55 feet
The name also refers to an older route which began on the
rock to the left of Golden Staircase and diagonaled right
towards the top of the cliff; crossing onto Nubble Face
near the bottom, ending at the top down stream end of
Nubble Face. The name refers to a large oak which used
to overhang the cliff and cover it with golden catkins.

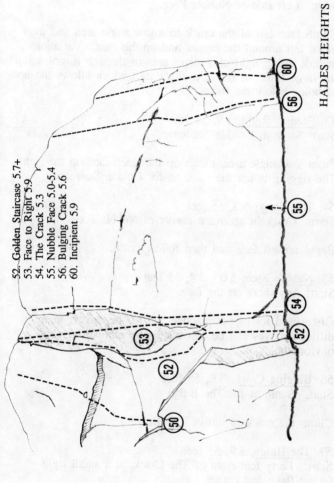

52. Golden Staircase 5.7+
53. Face to Right 5.9
54. The Crack 5.3
55. Nubble Face 5.0-5.4
56. Bulging Crack 5.6
60. Incipient 5.9

Start: Left side of Nubble Face.

Climb face left of the crack to a low angle area and then move left around the corner and up the face. Variations include going right of a silver area or through it, not using the large flake, or doing a direct start which allows the use of holds below the flake.

53. <u>Face to Right</u>, 5.9, 55 feet
Start: Same as Golden Staircase

From low angle area, climb up the steep face on the right. The rigging is not the same as for Golden Staircase.

54. <u>The Crack</u>, 5.3, 55 feet
Start: Crack in upstream corner of Nubble Face.

Begin up left face and then follow crack.

55. <u>Nubble Face</u>, 5.0 - 5.4, 55 feet
Start: Anywhere on the face.

Often used for rappel practice and for beginners, many difficult moves can be constructed by eliminating the obvious holds.

56. <u>Bulging Crack</u>, 5.6, 55 feet
Start: Same as for The Bulge

Climb the crack to left of The Bulge.

57. <u>The Bulge</u>, 5.9, 55 feet
Start: Forty feet right of The Crack, at a small right facing flake and corner.

56

Ascend the corner and climb the bulge directly. Use neither the crack nor the right edge.

58. Friction Layback, 5.6, 55 feet
Start: Same as The Bulge.

Ascend flake system on the right side of The Bulge.

59. Walk On By, 5.10+, 55 feet
Start: Same as Incipient.

Climb the face between Incipient and Friction Layback. A contrived but worthwhile climb in which all large and good handholds are not used.

60. Incipient, 5.9, 55 feet
Start: Ten feet right of The Bulge below a small crack in the overhang.

Climb up the face to pull the overhang at the incipient crack and follow the crack to the top. Use only holds up to six inches from the crack. F.A. Bob Evans and Chips Janger in 1969.

61. Crucifixion, 5.10+, 55 feet
Start: Same as Incipient.

Climb to the overhang and pull it using handholds 4 feet right of Incipient. This is done by using underclings and pinches to pull onto the face above. This is a one move problem which leaves one in a crucifix position.

62. Chris' Goat, 5.7, 55 feet
This climb is named after Chris Scoredos, who began climbing as a boy in Colorado and then moved to the

Washington, D.C. area in the forties. From 1944-45 he was Chairman of the Trail Club Council. Chris was a prolific climber with ascents in many of the mountain ranges in the West and in Canada. He had a master's degree in Biology, then got a degree in Law, and spent his life as a business man. He is remembered for always showing up to climb, rain or shine.

Start: Same as Incipient.

Climb to overhang, move right to the edge and continue to the top.

63. Crippling Paralysis, 5.10+, 55 feet
Start: Same as Cripple's Crack.

Friction on the face just left of the crack with holds from Chris' Goat and Cripple's Crack off route.

64. Cripple's Crack, 5.10, 55 feet
A tension lead was attempted here in the 1940's, and because of the zippering of the pitons the climb was known as Pincushion.

Start: Around the right corner of Nubble Face at the foot of a system of cracks.

Follow the prominent left crack all the way up.

65. Cripple's Face, 5.9, 55 feet
This portion of the rock was referred to as Cripple's Delight at one time. Tom Evans and Mike Nicholson were working on this climb in the late sixties when Evans strained his shoulder on it and hence the name.

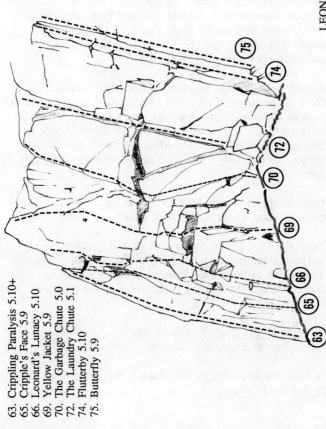

LEONARD'S LUNACY

Start: To the right of Cripple's Crack, about 3 feet.

Climb face to the right of the prominent crack, without using the right edge. Good form will save arm wear.

66. <u>Leonard's Lunacy</u>, 5.10, 55 feet
It was considered a lunacy for Richard Leonard to suggest that this was a route. Donald Hubbard made the ascent in 1943. It was first led by Herb Conn in 1945 using 3 pitons. Originally, this climb escaped left onto what is now the top of Cripple's (5.8).

Richard Leonard was an attorney from San Fransisco, active in the Sierra Club, who climbed in Yosemite and in Western Canada. When the war began he came to D.C. and worked for the Army Quartermaster Corps where he developed equipment for the Mountaineering and Ski Troops. In the early 1940's he helped develop the nylon rope.

Start: Right of Cripple's, scramble to an off balance ledge below a white streak in the rock above.

Climb the face left of the groove onto the ramp. Undercling the overhang; step right and pull the overhang using a thin right crack. Reach high for this with a balance move. The rigging is the same as for Make A Wish.

67. <u>Wish Come True</u>, 5.11+, 55 feet
Start: Same as Leonard's Lunacy.

Layback the left edge of the Make a Wish face with feet staying on the face.

68. <u>Make A Wish</u>, 5.10, 55 feet
Start: Same as Yellow Jacket.

Climb up the groove stemming wide, between Leonard's
Lunacy and Yellow Jacket, like a wishbone. Half way up,
step left and follow a thin crack to the top. Several hard
variations can be done here.

69. <u>Yellow Jacket</u>, 5.9, 55 feet
Start: Right of Leonard's Lunacy below an overhanging
block.

Climb over or around the block to a ledge. Climb the
diagonal groove past the yellow spot.

70. <u>The Garbage Chute</u>, 5.0, 55 feet
Start: Large corner 20 feet right of Cripple's.

Climb up the corner.

71. <u>Chris Wex Don Traverse</u>
Named after Chris Scoredos, Arnold Wexler and Donald
Hubbard, this was a classic traverse in the 1940's and
50's.

Donald Hubbard began climbing in the 1940's. He worked
at the National Bureau of Standard for 39 years,
researching the sensitivity of silver bromide for
photographic emulsions. His lab has been cited for
making major contributions to photography in this century.
He lives in the area, and is still active in the outdoors.
He said of himself that he was never a climbing enthusiast
as some of the others at that time, but "once you are a
character, you can't let the public down." Those who

61

Arnold Wexler and Don Jacobs on the Chris Wex Don
Traverse (Wexler)

know him, and have heard him yodel at the top of the cliff, can only agree.

Start: Climb partially up The Garbage Chute.

Traverse 400 feet right to the end of the cliff. Continue around the backside of the cliff until the ground is reached.

72. The Laundry Chute, 5.1, 45 feet
Start: Follow the narrow chute 10 feet to the right of the corner of Garbage Chute.

This climb was formerly named Suction Cup Corner. The large block in front of the cliff is now used for bouldering and was called Key Climb by Sterling Hendricks in 1945 who "furnished the key and the name."

73. Serenity Syndrome, 5.11-, 45 feet
Start: The right face of the corner 8 feet left of Easy Layback.

Edge up the piton scars, using the left edge minimally and not reaching far around the edge. F.A. John Bercaw.

74. Flutterby, 5.10, 45 feet
Start: At the corner 8 feet left of Easy Layback.

With the feet on Butterfly and the hands on Serenity, climb the face to the top. F.A. Chris Kulczycki.
75. Butterfly, 5.9, 45 feet
Start: At the corner 8 feet left of Easy Layback.

Climb the very thin face by the corner without using holds in the corner or on Serenity. A 5.11 finish can be done.

63

When standing on the ledge before the top, continue straight up without using the nubbins one foot from the corner and not using the edge on the right.

76. <u>Merv's Nerve</u>, 5.10, 45 feet
This climb is named after Mervel Olsen.

Start: Between Butterfly and Easy Layback, 5 feet left of Easy Layback.

Climb up the thin face between corner and crack; avoid holds used on Butterfly and Easy Layback. The obvious flake is off route as is the major hold to the left. The top of the route is a grade harder for short folks.

77. <u>Easy Layback</u>, 5.4, 45 feet
Start: Prominent crack 20 feet right of the corner formed by The Garbage Chute.

Follow crack to the top, not always as a layback.

78. <u>Eliminates</u>, 5.7, 45 feet
Start: Right of Easy Layback.

Climb the face to the right of the Easy Layback crack.

79. <u>Fingernail</u>, 5.10, 50 feet
Start: Below hairline crack right of Easy Layback.

Follow crack to the top.

80. <u>Zig Zag</u>, 5.12-, 50 feet
Start: Below a double Z shaped crack between Triple A and Fingernail.

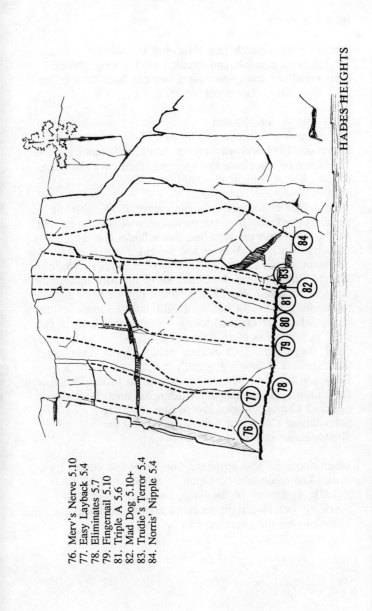

HADES HEIGHTS

76. Merv's Nerve 5.10
77. Easy Layback 5.4
78. Eliminates 5.7
79. Fingernail 5.10
81. Triple A 5.6
82. Mad Dog 5.10+
83. Trudie's Terror 5.4
84. Norris' Nipple 5.4

Smear up the smooth face following the hairline zig zags as closely as possible and keeping off the large flakes. Two variations have been done, one has been called One Step Two Step. Don't use anything big!

81. <u>Triple A</u>, 5.6, 50 feet
The route was first climbed by Arnold Wexler in December 1943 and was named Arnold's Arduous Ascent. The name of the climb has been modified over the years to first A.A.A. and finally Triple A.

Arnold Wexler has been climbing since 1941. Sterling Hendricks was his frequent partner in mountaineering and taught him much on trips into the Selkirks and the Canadian Rockies. Wexler has written a very mathematical article on the Theory of Belaying. While Donald Hubbard was the Chairman of the Mountaineering Section, he asked Wexler and Herb Conn to write a guide to climbing at Carderock, which documented many of the routes which are climbed today. Wexler still lives in the area, though he is often seen at Seneca where he used to climb frequently. First ascents include Conns East Direct Start (graded at 5.6, it's actually much harder) and Ye Gods and Little Fishes (5.8). In addition to all the major and minor cliffs around the Washington area, he has also explored Champe Rocks, the Nelson Rocks and Schoolhouse Cave near Seneca W.V., and the Shawangunks in New Paltz N.Y.

Start: About 15 feet upstream from an inside corner by a crack. The climb can be begun as a mantle or as a left layback, to the top of the flake. Move up beneath an overhang, continue right on small knobs directly to the top. Variations on the overhang can be done.

82. <u>Mad Dog</u>, 5.10+, 50 feet
Start: Below the bolt between Triple A and the corner.

Climb the face between Triple A and Trudie's Terror. The upper portion originally went left but the climb can be made more difficult by staying right, closer to Trudie's Terror. F.A. Tom Blevins.

83. <u>Trudie's Terror</u>, 5.4, 50 feet
Named after Trudie Nicholson, wife of Mike Nicholson, who displayed the common beginner fears when put on this route when she did it in 1966.

Start: Inside corner furthest downstream before the rocks protrude into the river.

Climb up the corner crack either jamming or stemming.

84. <u>Norris's Nipple</u>, 5.4, 55 feet
A one move problem, this was first climbed by June Lehman. June started climbing when she was in her fifties and climbed actively from 1966 to the mid seventies. She is still seen climbing today. She named the route after noting the profile's resemblance to Bob Norris' pectorals. Bob Norris taught at the Potomac Valley Climbing School and was June Lehman's climbing friend and coach. He is said to have responded with "you wouldn't dare" when he heard of the climb's name.

Start: Same as Trudie's Terror.

Move right and then up the bump which gave the climb its name. A variation can be done which climbs the bulging wall between Trudie's and Norris'

85. <u>Photogenic</u>, 5.6, 60 feet
Start: Between Trudie's Terror and Sterling's Twin
Cracks.

Climb up from the river through the bulge and to the top.
F.A. Larry Griffin 1967.

86. <u>Sterling's Twin Cracks</u>, 5.8, 60 feet
Start: In the dry summer, when the river drops to expose
the bank, walk beyond Trudie's Terror to the base of a
crack. Two routes were done here: Sterling's North
Crack (5.8) follows left leaning corner until one can follow
the upstream crack to the top. Sterling's South Crack
(5.8) goes up the corner and face adjacent to the corner,
until one reaches the downstream crack. Follow this crack
to the top.

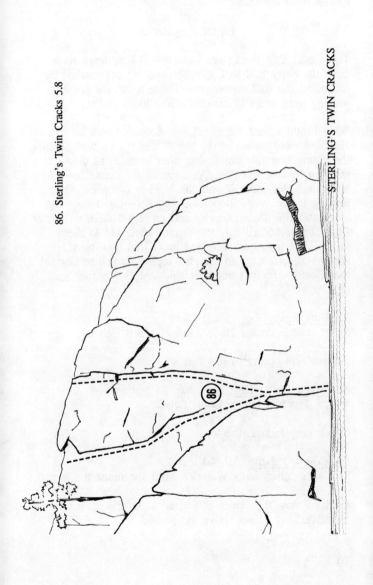

86. Sterling's Twin Cracks 5.8

STERLING'S TWIN CRACKS

Easter Egg Rocks

The Easter Egg Rocks are located 400 feet down river from the entry trail to Carderock and are approached by following the trail downriver. These rocks are not as heavily used and still contain a few loose flakes.

"One bright Easter Sunday, Chris Scoredos and Donald Hubbard were sitting at the top of the Spider Walk, letting the young hopefuls down, one after another, as they fell off. Finally one rebelled. 'You grandpa's, come down here and climb this thing if you can.' They complied, then turning to the young hopefuls, they apologized for overestimating their maturity and promised them an Easter Egg Hunt. Accordingly the group proceeded to these cliffs. The grandpas then tied in as lead men on their ropes and took eggs to the cliff tops. They then taunted those below, for not one was able to follow either lead..." (*Up Rope*, 1947).

87. <u>Pink Easter Egg</u>, 5.2, 30 feet
Start: Inside corner 20 feet left of Court Echelle.

Scramble in corner to the top.

88. <u>Green Easter Egg</u>, 5.2 - 5.6, 35 feet
Start: Ten feet left of Court Echelle.

Climb easy face to the top.

89. <u>Courte Echelle</u>, 5.9, 40 feet
This was called Jan's Waterloo until she made the ascent.

Start: Below the center of Scoredos' Overhang, a four foot overhang 5 feet above the ground.

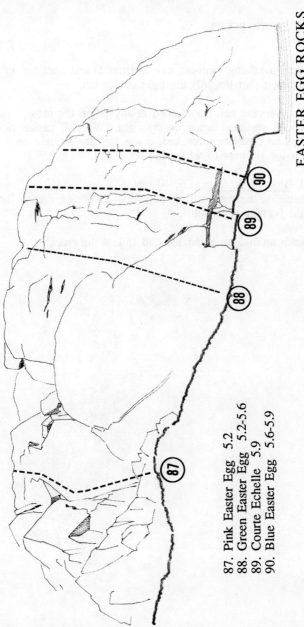

EASTER EGG ROCKS

87. Pink Easter Egg 5.2
88. Green Easter Egg 5.2-5.6
89. Courte Echelle 5.9
90. Blue Easter Egg 5.6-5.9

Climb overhang (without any assistance) and continue to the top, either towards the right or the left.

The overhang can be climbed at any point, the most difficult variation being on the right. With all variations a frog-like position is reached as the feet are brought up over the lip near to where the hands are.

90. <u>Blue Easter Egg</u>, 5.6, 40 feet
Start: At the right end of Scoredos' Overhang on the far right portion of the cliff.

Climb around the overhang and follow the crack.

Jam Box

To reach the Jam Box, walk downstream along the path from Carderock. At the second gully, approximately 500 feet from Carderock, walk towards the river. The cliff is upriver.

91. <u>Jan's Chimney</u>, 5.8, 30 feet
Start: A flared chimney facing downstream.

The difficulty can be varied so as to do a nice chimney or to struggle with an off-width chimney. The face can also be climbed, as can variations such as feet on one wall and hands on the other.

92. <u>Jam Box</u>, 5.10, 30 feet
A remarkable feat of the time, this was first climbed in August of 1951 by Tony Soler. Soler worked at the National Bureau of Standards and then at the Navy Ordinance Lab. Climbs at Seneca and Devil's Tower are named after him, as well as at Camp Lewis. Tony Soler also made his own scuba gear, which he frequently used when the Mountaineering Section climbed at Great Falls. A critical handhold has broken off at the top, which was given as a gift to Ed Worrel, who was working on the climb at that time.

Start: Climb jam box to a platform, (or take an easier approach to the ledge by going right).

Then do the impossible, proceed up through the grungy gap. This usually requires a knee jam.

Don Jacobs, Arnold Wexler, and Chris Scoredos in Jan's Chimney. Could this be how Chris got so short? (Conns, ca. 1944)

74

The photographer has to climb too. Don Hubbard and his trusty Brownie camera. (Conns ca. 1944)

93. <u>The Last Great Problem</u>, 35 feet
Start: Overhanging wall left of the Jam Box.

This awaits a free ascent.

94. <u>Novice</u>, 5.0, 35 feet
Start: Below a right facing corner on the face around the left corner of Jam Box.

This is a good beginner's face. It is also blocky enough to learn the placement of protection for lead climbing.

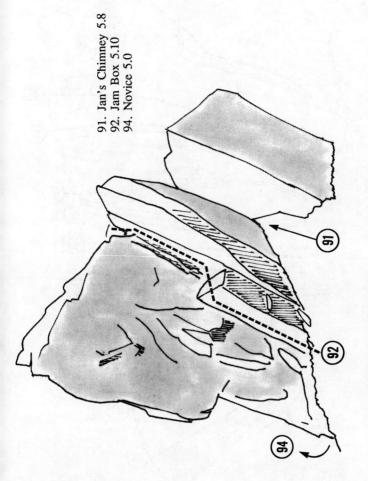

91. Jan's Chimney 5.8
92. Jam Box 5.10
94. Novice 5.0

JAM BOX

CAMP LEWIS

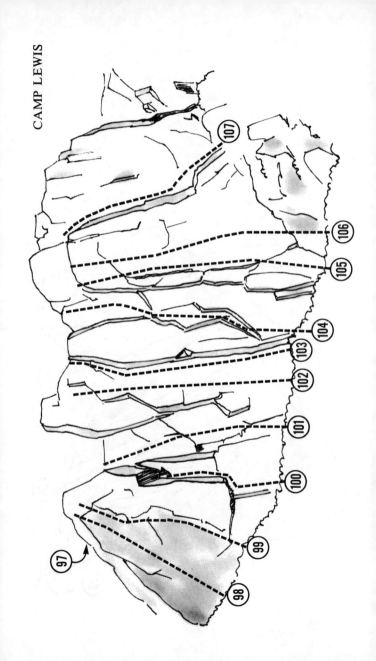

Camp Lewis

Camp Lewis, or Lewis Rocks, are opposite Boucher Rocks, and are located on the Maryland side of the Potomac River 200 yards upstream from I-495. From Carderock walk down the C & O Canal towpath 1 mile to a spillway. A marker for this turn off into the woods is the long building on the other side of the canal which ends about where the turnoff towards the river is. Follow the stream to an intersection with another spillway. Cross this and walk right to the river. The cliffs are downstream. From the parking lot at Lock 10, the walk on the towpath is about the same distance. From Lock 10 walk upstream along the towpath, passing under the Beltway, and to the spillway.

Although not as impressive as the rocks at Boucher or at Carderock, this small crag has an assortment of awkward climbs and plenty of bouldering. Because the rock faces south to south west, good cold weather climbing can be found here.

The first large block downstream from the spillway has the climb The Shadow. The next rock downstream is called

---

Routes for map on page 78

the Dome. Then come the Main Cliffs. A steep
walkdown separates them from the Mam Cliffs, and
beyond these is the East Face. The names suggest more
rock than really exists.

95. The Shadow, 5.10, 25 feet
Start: On the first large face downstream from the
spillway entry to the river, upriver from the main section
of the cliff.

Climb up the right side of the block using the crack and
then move left and up.

96. The Dome
Frequently scrambled on in the forties, this low vegetated
dome has no long face to rig a climb on, but is a good
boulder block and resting spot.

97. Willy Nilly Traverse
In February 1946 Donald Hubbard wrote a short verse
about a pleasant day at Camp Lewis. During this time the
group was learning about wilderness survival and what
foods could be obtained from the wilds. The characters
are Delores Alley and Sally Chambers, two enlisted women
assigned to the area, Donald Hubbard and Arnold Wexler:

> "It may sound absurd
> But Alley and Sally
> Climbed Willy and Nilly
> While Donald and Arnold
> Looked silly and chilly
> Cooking a pot herb."

Start: At the top left portion of the main section of the
cliff.

Following a horizontal ledge, cross over the face and around to the more broken section of the cliff. Keep traversing all the way past the Jam Crack and then escape left up the Lizard's Ledge.

98. <u>Crawford's Crash</u>, 5.9, 20 feet
Start: Face on the upriver side of the main cliff.

A thin balance climb with a potential swing around the corner.

99. <u>Friction Dome</u>, 5.10, 25 feet
Start: Begin on the nose.

Place a foot on the ledge and climb up the edge.

100. <u>Ferocious Layback</u>, 5.6, 30 feet
Start: Under the pinnacle.

Climb up the crack beginning by the overhang and continue to the pinnacle. If done strictly as a layback, 5.9. This has been called West Sentinal.

101. <u>Beginner's Notch</u>, 5.0, 30 feet
Start: The blocky cliff between Ferocious Layback and the blank wall.

102. <u>Schaefer's Aching Back</u>, 5.11, 35 feet
Start: On blank wall downstream from Ferocious Layback.

Up a thin crack in the middle of a smooth face. Change cracks near the top. This was originally put up as an aid climb.

Scrambling at Camp Lewis (Vos)

103. <u>Shipley's Climb</u>, 5.10, 35 feet
Start: At Schaefer's Aching Back.

Follow the thin right crack up.

104. <u>Pony Express</u>, 5.6, 30 feet
Start: On a right facing slope.

The crux is getting off of the ground onto the slope.
Scramble to the top.

105. <u>Jam Crack</u>, 5.9, 30 feet
A large loose block forms the left hand edge of this climb.
The beginning of this climb has been called Short Man's
Climb.

Start: Below the crack in the face 15 feet left of the
walkdown separating the cliff from Mam Cliff.

Climb the awkward crack. The block on the bottom left
has been called Short Man's Climb, and for a short person
offers a boulder problem to get to the top.

106. <u>Norris' Downfall</u>, A1, 30 feet
Start: Rurp crack 8 feet right of Jam Crack.

107. <u>Lizard's Ledge</u>, 5.1, 20 feet
Start: At the walkdown between the main rocks and the
Mam Cliffs.

Climb up the right sloping ledges to the top.
This was a favorite scramble of the fifties.

108. <u>No Horror</u>, 5.1, 20 feet
Start: On the very short downstream edge of the walkdown.

Climb up the protruding flakes.

109. <u>Junior Horror</u>, 5.7, 30 feet
Start: Left of the crack.
Climb the face without using the crack to the left of the face. A 5.4 variation can be done on the right side of the crack.

110. <u>East Face</u>, 5.6, 20 feet
This face was frequently climbed in the 1940's.

Start: A short south-east facing wall 100 feet downstream of the Mam Cliffs.

Climb the slightly overhanging wall. If necessary, it can be started on the right ledge.

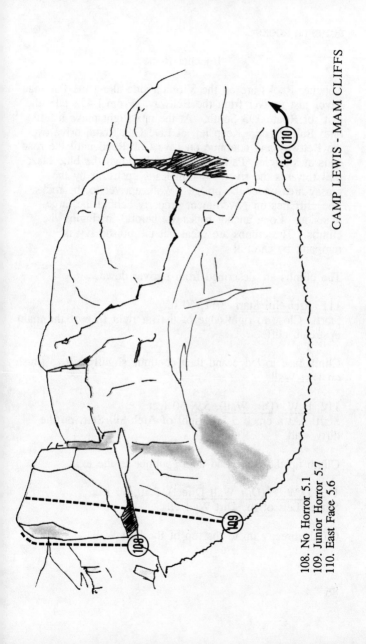

CAMP LEWIS - MAM CLIFFS

108. No Horror 5.1
109. Junior Horror 5.7
110. East Face 5.6

to 110

Boucher Rocks

Boucher Rocks are on the Virginia side along the Potomac
River just upriver from the Beltway. From I-495 take the
exit for Route 193 South. At the next light make a left
onto Balls Road. Keep left at Live Oak Road, drive over
the Beltway and continue on Live Oak Road until the road
ends at a circle. Park here and walk down the blue blaze
trail towards the river. A trail leads upstream by the
grassy area under the bridge. Walk upriver to the rocks.
The cliff lies on government property behind the large
mansion. Long anchor ropes are helpful in rigging the
climbs. The climbs are great but the poison ivy is
rampant; be careful!

The climbs are described from upriver down.

111. <u>Arch-Sill Start</u>, 5.11, 50 feet
Start: Close to right edge of the far right face of the main
upstream cliff.

Climb face to ledge and then continue slightly left to finish
on Dirt Wall.

112. <u>D.W.</u> (<u>Dirt Wall</u>), 5.9, 50 feet
Start: At a crack 5 feet right of Arch-Sill Start on the
dirty wall.

Climb up the crack and then continue to the top.

113. <u>D.W.D.</u> (<u>Dirt Wall Direct</u>), 5.10, 50 feet
Start: Left of the Dirt Wall crack.

Climb directly up to the top of the Dirt Wall.

114. <u>Dirty Dancing</u>, 5.10+, 50 feet
Start: At flake right of Long Corner.

Climb up flake and continue on face to ascend upper wall.

115. <u>Long Corner</u>, 5.8, 50 feet
Start: Start below a large right facing corner.

Climb up the main corner, staying in the corner to the top.
It is also possible to layback the corner right of the corner
in the cliff (5.5) or the left side of this protrusion. The
variation continues up to the right of the corner on the
face. Once on the ledge the crux of the climb is to finish
directly. Another variation begins to the left of the corner
and goes up the face (5.9).

116. <u>Dancing Climb</u>, 5.8, 40 feet
First climbed by Paul Bradt in 1946, the name is thought
to refer to Bradt's appearance: first one end up, then the
other, like a measuring worm dancing.

If Gustave Gambs is to be called the grandfather of
climbing in the area, then Paul Bradt is the father of local
climbing. He was introduced to climbing by Gus Gambs
and formed the core of the group of what was to become
the Mountaineering Section. He was the first to have the
idea of practicing belaying with a dummy rigged a system
in his yard--a forerunner of Oscar. Paul and his wife Jo
were editors of *Up Rope* from 1945-47.
Paul worked with mass spectrometry at the National
Bureau of Standards.

Start: At the base of a short cliff below a low angle
slab/face, 20 feet left of Long Corner.

BOUCHER ROCKS

Climb up to the base of the slab, giving this climb its other name. Friction up the slope not using the right edge. A variation called Scarface can be climbed further left (5.10).

117. <u>Seeds and Stems</u>, 5.10, 40 feet
Start: Same as Dancing Climb.

From the base of the slab, climb the right facing corner, stemming around the overhang. Knowing that the name refers to marijuana, one can guess the era in which it was first climbed.

118. <u>Twin Cracks</u>, 5.9, 45 feet
Start: Around the buttress and up the hill 35 yards from the main section of the cliff at the base of two cracks.

Climb up between the cracks, beginning with a mantle and ending with the crux. A low angle wall here has also been climbed.

Routes for map on page 88.

Other Cliffs in the Area

Although not as accessible and not as high, these cliffs have been scouted by various generations of climbers.

Vaso Island

The wooded island across from Carderock is Vaso Island, though it is usually called Herzog Island by climbers. In the summer it is possible to wade over on the upriver section by the bend in the river. The main section of cliffs lies on the south side with up to 60 feet high rock. There are many routes, a few of which will be mentioned because their names have been recorded. Other routes will be left unnamed so that there will always be "new" routes to do.

Names historically given to routes on the island, but for which no positive route is now known, include Fingertip Balance Climb, with Knubble Face and The Crack With No Name downstream from it; Inside Corner Climb; Arnold's Overhang; Hornet's Nest Climb; Superman's Roof; and Leonard's Tenison Corner.

119. <u>Reality Island</u>, 5.10, 35 feet
Start: On the upriver side of the island near the summer wading spot.

Follow thin crack on overhanging wall.

120. <u>Reality Arete</u>, 5.10, 35 feet
Start: Same as Reality Island.

Climb to the right of Reality Island.

121. <u>Backdoor Man</u>, 5.9+, 40 feet
Start: Large crack opposite the cliffs at Carderock.

Towards the middle of the island a series of cliffs offer
numerous face climbs (5.5-5.9) as well as an overhang
(5.10) and crack climbs (5.8). Jan's Semi Chimney is the
crack with a small cave at the base. The corner crack
climb left of the overhang, in a recess behind Jan's Semi
Chimney, is the Upside Down Climb (5.8).

122. <u>Chairman's Chimney</u>, 5.8, 40 feet
The climb is more appropriately called Chairmen's
Chimney because the first people to climb it were the
chairman and former chairmen of the Mountaineering
Committee: Sterling Hendricks (first ascent in September
1943), Paul Bradt, Donald Hubbard, and Chris Scoredos.
In the following years, it was tradition for Section
Chairpersons to do this climb once during their
appointment.

Start: Prominent "V" shaped chimney about 150 yards
downstream from the middle section of the cliff before a
gully. It is not visible until one looks directly down the
chimney. Access to the bottom is easiest by rappelling or
climbing down the gully through the vines.

Stem up to a crucial triangular hold. Chimney the rest, or
use the face holds. It is also possible to diagonal up the
layback at the bottom and then traverse into the V.

One of the first tension climbs completed in the area:
Dick Leonard on a corner climb on the south side of
Herzog Island (Wexler).

Further downstream, across from the rocks on Turkey Island, is a large face above the water, called Herzog's Face, which offers moderate face climbing.

Turkey Island

A climb known as Mole Hill has been done, though no record exists as to its location.

Prospect and Maddox Rock

Both these areas are approached by walking upstream along the river from Boucher Rock. Access otherwise would be through private property. The climbs The Beak, The Cave Climb, and The Chimney Climb have been done at Prospect Rock, which is located a half mile west of the mouth of Bullneck Run. This area was scouted by Gustave Gambs who also scouted Maddox Rock which is about a third of a mile east of Prospect Rock. Maddox Rock has a wall for face climbing and traversing and a semi cave.

Eagle Rock

This is just upriver from Boucher and is a short cliff with interesting cracks. Eagle's Beak and West Face are two recorded climbs.

Himes Island

Tatge's Terrible Tussle is the only recorded climb on this island. Eleanor Tatge climbed frequently in the 1940's with the Conns; she nows lives in Florida.

Quaking Aspen

This is the cliff by Chain Bridge: it is a fairly tall cliff, but like most of these areas the rock is either rotten or vegetated. This is the local location for climbers to practice piton craft.

Ripe Mango

Park at the overlook just west of Hazel Run on the George Washington Parkway, VA. This is the first overlook after Key Bridge, approximately 3 miles west of Key bridge and 2 miles east of Chain Bridge. Walk 300 yards along the parkway to the top of the climb. There is a good anchor tree, though it is best to get a belay while rigging the climb. The descent route is a pathway down by a concrete culvert which goes under the Parkway. This quarried cliff is 70 feet high but has loose rock.

123. Ripe Mango, 5.10+, 70 feet
Start: A shallow left facing inside corner.

Climb corner till half height, then hand traverse left. The crux is to continue up the vertical crack.

The Direct Mango (A.2-A.3) nails the incipient crack up to the free-climb of Ripe Mango. The rock is fragile.

Boulder Problems
Art Powell

Bouldering is one of the best things about Carderock.
Most of the hardest climbing is right off the ground. This
is mainly due to the fact that the rock is steepest there.
Although what follows is a brief guide to some of its more
well-known problems, the reader is encouraged to find his
or her own. Just pick any area of rock and climb up
about ten feet. Then make it harder and harder by
eliminating holds. The possibilities are endless.

Boulder problems listed for the main areas are from West
to East or Left to Right as you face the rocks.

Main Area

B1. First move of The Flake, 5.10
Even though the climb is named after a higher move, this
one is at least as hard. Find the climb called The Flake.
Ascend until the right foot leaves first hold, then traverse
off left or right.

B2. First move of Eight Ball, 5.11
This move used to be a little easier but the first hold for
the left hand went from flat and horizontal to thin and
vertical. Use the aforementioned hold to layback left until
the right foot is on a horizontal crack about three feet off
the ground. Harder for short people.

B3. Jan's Block
A mundane problem but good for arm strength: begin on
the large block in front of Jan's Face. On the higher end
reach to a large flake. Place the right foot on a sloping
face, balance the right hand on a right flake and reach to

the top. Now traverse downstream. The traverse can also be completed without using the upper edge. Many variations exist, including one on the left side which is used for mantle practice. A two handed mantle: grab the top edge, dangle the feet and pull up not using any footholds. If doing a left or right handed mantle, the feet are "allowed" to smear on the rock.

B4. The Circle
Start on the far right side of Jan's Face using holds of Elsie's Other. Pull up on an undercling, work the feet and hands up until the left foot can get onto the green face. This is a very committing boulder problem. Using the right edge continue up and reach to a bomber hold with the left hand. Continue left, then down, placing the feet and then the hands in a left facing crescent. Continue down and right, placing the hands in an undercling. Traverse right to the edge under the overhang where the boulder problem began. Continue either using the initial undercling or go below these holds (this leaves one in a humorous position, struggling and scrunching an inch off of the ground). The travese can also be done from right to left.

B5. Angled Layback, 5.11
This problem will teach you good balance. Find the crack that angles left just to the left of The X. Layback up the crack using only footholds and handholds in the crack.

B6. Easy Mantle, 5.9
Find large flat handholds about six feet off the ground and about three to four feet from the right edge of Barnacle Face. Mantle on the left arm and place the right foot next to the left hand. Stand up without using any holds higher than the starting ledge.

B7. <u>Hard Mantle</u>, 5.11
At first it is difficult to believe this goes, but it's easy
with enough practice. Using fingernail holds about 6' off
the ground just right of the corner, smear right foot just
below large foothold (completely off route) and smear left
foot in small u-shaped indentation. Move right foot to
small nub just above the aforementioned right foothold and
mantle on the left hand. Reach up to small knob near
edge with right hand. Change mantel hand to face
upstream and place left foot on small nub 3" below and
left of the hand. Now stand up and grab huge flake next
to the rock's edge with the left hand.

B8. <u>Mickey Mantle</u>, 5.9
Just below downstream end of Impossible Face Traverse
about eight feet left of the Sloth. Mantle the large knob
about 5' off the deck.

B9. <u>No Hands</u>
Start at the detached rock at the base of the cliff 10 feet
to the right of the Sloth. Three variations are possible:
start at the bottom at the right end. Without using the
hands walk up the edge placing the feet 1 inch from the
edge. It is also possible to start at the bottom of the
diagonal, moving up right placing the feet very closely to
the underside of the diagonal. Follow to the top with no
hands. The third variation starts on the left end at a semi-
detached rock. Follow the steep right edge to the top,
without using the hands and keeping the feet one inch
from the edge.

B10. <u>Upstream Side of Walk-Down</u>, 5.10, committing!
Find 10' overhanging rock which angles up and right. Use
edge and backside holds to ascend.

Use a pushbutton grip finger pull up and dynamic reach to the horn. Poor landing. A variation can be done with the horn off route (5.11).

B11. One Arm Mantle, 5.9
Just right of long vertical crack to the right of Golden Staircase. This is another neat balance problem. Put your left hand on the big knob and mantle it. Put the right foot just below the hand and stand up keeping the left hand on the mantle. The right hand is kept behind the back and not used at all.

B12. Real Hard, 5.11
One of the harder classic problems in the main area. In the middle of the bulge just right of the One Arm Mantle. Use left fingernails on a horizontal and fingertips on nubs for the right. Shorter people stand on the root. Stand on right foot. Get left foot purchase. Grab large knob about eight feet off deck. Although exhiliarating the next moves get you up pretty high. Traverse off left.

B13. Undercling, 5.10
Just to the right of Real Hard is a crack with an undercling which slants up to the right. Place your foot on the obvious large foothold below the crack. With no other holds, stand up.

B14. Left of Corner, 5.11
Just to the left of the corner between Incipient Crack and Cripples is a smooth bulging face. Climb it.

B15. Four Variations on Classic Block, 5.8-5.11
Without a doubt the best bouldering rock at Carderock. This large block is to the right of Cripples. It contains four classic boulder problems.

Variation 1: On the left face, grab the two pinches above the small overhang and climb to the top.

Variation 2: On the front face, grab the obvious right hand hold and grab the flake layback style above the small overhang. Use the outermost triangular left foothold for the easiest variation.

Variation 3: To make Variation 2 much harder use the tiny left foothold right of the one used in Variation 2.

Variation 4: For the ultimate finger tester, move both hands onto finger pinches inside the original two handholds.

(It is also possible to do a one handed mantle from the right side.)

B16. Thumb Pinch, 5.10
Just to the right of Four Variations is a very esoteric layback problem. Find a small triangular foothold which angles up for the left foot. Grab the large layback handhold about three feet off the ground with the right hand and find a small nub just below it for the right foot. The left hand goes high to an angled crack that can be grasped in a number of interesting ways. Stand up and climb to the top.

B17. Undercling, 5.10
Another classic Carderock boulder problem. Just left of Butterfly outside corner, grab the large obvious undercling with both hands and climb to the ledge. Exit to the left. (Note: to make this a little tougher, keep both feet inside the vertical fault on the left side.

B18. <u>Jackhammer</u>, 5.10
Grab the two obvious high handholds on the outside edge
of the arete. Use any footholds you can find and mantle
onto the right arm.

B19. <u>Fingernail</u>, 5.10
The hardest move on Fingernail as with many Carderock
climbs is the first one. Find the horizontal ridge. Put
your hands on the left side of the vertical crack. Find the
nubbin foothold on the left side of the veritcal crack. Step
up to it with your left foot and then put your right foot on
the right side of the horizontal ridge next to your hands.
Stand up with no other holds above the ridge.

B20. Three Variations of <u>Triple A</u>, 5.8-5.10

Variation 1: Place both hands on the obvious horizontal
holds. Climb until your feet are on the ledge where your
hands started. Use the obvious hold up and right to stand
up.

Variation 2 and 3: Treat the problem as a pure mantle
and do it with your left foot as the first to reach the ledge
(easier) and then the right.

Traverses

B21. <u>West Long Traverse</u>
A favorite Carderock warm-up. Start at the arete on the
outside of Impossible face. Traverse Impossible face and
round the overhanging corner onto the back wall. Traverse
the back wall in both directions, recross Impossible face
and then cross the Barnacle face. On the left side of the
Barnacle face, climb up and stem to the high back wall.

Cross this wall starting at an obvious horizontal ledge on the right side. At the left side of this wall, reverse and return to the starting point. Note: It is possible to extend this traverse even further to the east around the Sloth but the DZ (drop zone) is poor and the moves difficult.

B22. <u>Low Traverse</u>
It is possible to start at Trudie's Corner and traverse left up to the Carderock walkdown. There are three cruxes. The first is across Merv's Nerve face. The second crux is around Crippple's corner. Third is across the face just downstream from Golden Staircase and the last is under Spiderwalk. Note: It is easier to traverse the corner near Cripples about ten feet off the ground but the fall is a little unreasonable. Besides, the lower traverse is much more challenging!

B23. <u>One Arm Traverse</u>
A climber to remain unnamed figured out this traverse after he injured his left arm. Start just east of the big corner on a large left and a rounded right foothold both about a foot off the ground. Using your right hand only, traverse to the top of the block.

B24. <u>Over The Water</u>
Start at Trudie's Corner and traverse to the east as far as the rock goes. Careful, you'll get wet if you fall!

<u>Stannards Playground</u>
Take the path south of The Flake by Jan's Face toward the river.

B25. <u>Orangutang</u>
Find the face with the initials "TB" carved in the middle. On the right side a large protruding block on the right,

101

BOULDER PROBLEMS

find two high pull-up type holds. Do three successive rather long pull-ups without using your feet to ascend.

B26. <u>Over The Horn</u>
Climb up the middle of the TB wall until your left hand is using the bottom inside crack of the above mentioned protruding block as a laybak right hold. Reach around to the right and grab the right side of the block. Ascend straight up the middle of the block.

B27. <u>TB Wall</u>
Probably the easiest problem on this face. Climb right up the middle just left of the large protruding block.

B28. <u>Hard Layback</u>
Layback the right leaning crack as high as you can and then finish with a difficult jam.

B29. <u>Killer Corner</u>
Another classic hard boulder problem. Start on obvious handholds laybacking left. Climb the face any way you can after that. This one has several unique moves.

B30. <u>The Triangle</u>, 5.11+
Start: The Triangle refers to a large block located below the Canal about 20 feet upstream from the turn-off of the Billy Goat Trail to the Outlook Rocks. This is at the bend in the river and only a cleared step indicates the top of the small rock outcrop. A 6 foot 5.0 downclimb along the wall in the corner leads to a boulder problem. Continuing down the slope and right is a face with a triangular hole.

With the left edge off limits, the climb follows the crack up. The crux is then moving left and getting a foot into the triangle and continuing to the top.

Appendix

The Story of the Rocks
by John C. Reed, Jr.

The cracks, chimneys and nubbled faces of the cliffs at
Carderock are the products of a long and complicated
geologic history. The first part of the story concerns the
formation of the rocks that form the cliffs; the second
concerns the shaping of the cliffs themselves.

Early in its history, North America was part of a single
huge continent that also included the ancestral blocks of
Africa, Europe, and Asia. Between about 600 and 700
million years ago this mega-continent was broken and
slowly pulled apart to form an ocean referred to as Iapetus,
a forerunner of the present Atlantic. Between 550 and
about 470 million years ago movements of the plates
changed, and Iapetus began to close. As the ocean
progressively narrowed, chains of volcanic islands
developed along the margin of North America as oceanic
crust was pushed beneath the continent. The materials that
eventually were to from the rocks at Carderock were
deposited as mud and sand in a deep basin flanking one of
these island chains. Continued closure of the ocean
squeezed the islands against the edge of North America
about 450 million years ago. The soft sediments deposited
in the intervening basins were compressed and carried
downward, probably to depths of as much as 8 miles. As
a result the original sediments were deformed and the
minerals in them completely recrystallized to produce the
gnarled mica schist that forms the Carderock cliffs. Clay
minerals recrystallized to form mica, which tended to grow
with the individual flakes approximately perpendicular to

the direction in which the rocks were being compressed. This produced the conspicuous planar structure (schistosity) of the schist, which in the Carderock area trends slightly east of north and dips (slopes) west at angles of 60 to 75 degrees. At the same time, some of the quartz segregated to form pods and irregular knots ranging from fractions of an inch to several feet in diameter. These quartz segregations are irregularly distributed; commonly they occur in indistinct elongate groups that form lines of handholds such as those on Jan's Face and the Barnacle Face. These lines of quartz segregations and the long axes of the individual quartz knots probably mark the principal direction of stretching during formation of the schist. This direction lies in the plane of the schistosity and in the Carderock area it is generally inclined 10 to 20 degrees to the north. Planar fractures (joints) formed at various angles in the schist both during metamorphism and during subsequent uplift and cooling. Many of these lie about perpendicular to the schistosity and are vertical or dip steeply south.

The cliffs as we know them today are the products of much later chapters of geologic history. By about 300 million years ago, closure of the Iapetus Ocean was nearly complete, with the hump of Africa tucked against present U.S. mid-Atlantic coast and Europe fitted neatly against northern New England, Newfoundland, and Labrador. During this encounter, layers of sedimentary rocks originally deposited on the passive margin of North America as the ocean opened were deformed into the long series of parallel folds that form the present Appalachians. About 200 million years ago Africa began to pull away from North America once more, beginning the formation of the present Atlantic Ocean, and causing gradual subsidence of the eastern edge of North America. This was the beginning of a period of geologic stability along the eastern seaboard during which metamorphic rocks of the Piedmont, including the schists at Carderock, lay near the surface and were subject to prolonged weathering and near-surface decay. As the new Atlantic widened and weathering continued, the ancestral Potomac River began to cut its valley on the gently eastward sloping surface. As it crossed the weathered metamorphic rocks, it carved a broad, flat-floored valley much like the present valley between Seneca and Great Falls. Had conditions remained unchanged, there would have been no Carderock cliffs or other climbing areas along the Potomac gorge. The gorge and the flanking cliffs owe their existance to another set of geologic accidents.

During the Pleistocene, beginning about 1.6 million years ago, at least four major glaciations affected the northern hemisphere. Although glaciers never reached the Potomac valley, these glacial episodes played a critical role in the formation of the gorge and the Carderock cliffs. As water was withdrawn from the oceans to form glaciers, sea level fell dramatically. During each glaciation, rivers like the Potomac, whose valleys were delicately adjusted to the pre-glacial sea level, rapidly cut new channels in their lower valleys to adjust to the lower sea level at their mouths. The top of the cliffs at Carderock and the tips of the nearby islands are parts of a broad gravel-floored terrace that marks the floor of an early broad valley. The same terrace forms the top of Bear Island, and can be traced upstream to where it merges with the floor of the present valley above Great Falls. Great Falls marks the point where the river cascades from the floor of its old valley above the falls into the newly cut gorge below. Just how much of the gorge was cut during each of the Pleistocene glacial intervals is uncertain, but there are indications that the terrace at the tip of the Carderock cliffs is about 100,000 years old. If so, the cliffs as we know them today were shaped since then, probably largely during the last major glaciation 15,000-20,000 years ago.

The general architecture of the cliffs at Carderock is controlled by the joints and schistosity of the rocks, structures that were formed long before the gorge was carved. However, the texture of the rock and the character of the holds on any pitch depends on other factors. The rocks in the present cliffs are subject to chemical decay by trickling water laden with acids from decaying vegetation, to wedging by root growth or by ice freezing in cracks and fissures, to scouring by the silt-laden waters of the river during floods, and to wear and tear by myriad climbers. Chemical decay causes the breakdown of the individual mineral grains in the rock. Micaceous parts of the rock decay more readily than the quartz-rich parts, so that the quartz pods are gradually etched out to form nubbins. Scouring by flood waters tends to smooth the the rock and reduce or remove the nubbins. This is why the lower parts of many of the faces, which are scoured by floods every few years, tend to be smoother and more difficult than the upper parts, which are seldom flooded and where chemical decay has roughened the surfaces and etched the nubbins.

The rock texture also depends on how long a given face has been exposed to weathering and erosion. A face that is freshly exposed when a block or slab falls is smooth, while one that has been exposed for a long time is rough and studded with quartz nubbins. The character of a face climb also depends on whether the face is parallel to the schistosity of the rock or parallel to a joint that cuts across the schistosity. If it is parallel to schistosity, the holds are generally quartz nubbins separated by smooth expanses of schist (as on Jan's Face); if the face is at a high angle to the schistosity the rock is rougher and the holds may be the edges of small projecting flakes (as on the Swayback Layback) and the schist tends to be rough. Crack climbs such as the Spider Walk and Sterling's Crack are generally places where slabs or blocks have been partly wedged from the cliff face by frost or growing roots.

The cliffs at Carderock are the products of an amazing array of geological processes ranging from the movement of continents, the opening of oceans, and the spread of glaciers, to the delicate interplay of slow chemical weathering and scouring flood waters. They teach many lessons, one of which is that nothing is permanent, even the rocks! They will endure only a few million more years--enjoy them while you can!

Johnnie Reed (John C. Reed, Jr.) climbed with the Washington Rock Climbers and the PATC Mountaineering Section between 1947 and 1958. He served as editor of Up Rope and as chairman of the Mountaineering Section in 1952. He received a Ph.D. in geology from Johns Hopkins in 1954 and joined the U.S. Geological Survey. He has been involved in geologic studies in Shenandoah National Park, the Mount McKinley quadrangle, the Grandfather Mountain area in North Carolina, the Teton Range, the Leadville area in Colorado and the Sangre de Cristo Range in New Mexico. He has written popular accounts of the geology of the Blue Ridge, Great Falls and the Potomac Gorge, and the Teton Range. He currently lives in Golden, Colorado, and is involved in studies of the Precambrian rocks of Colorado and the preparation of the new geologic map of North America. He has been a member of the PATC since 1946 and is also an active member of the Colorado Mountain Club Whitewater Association.

The Return of Jam Crack Joe
by Jan Conn

When this song appeared in *Up Rope* in 1947, is writer
was Anonymous and the true identity of Jam Crack Joe
stimulated much conversation.

The Return of Jam Crack Joe

Tune: Little Joe The Wrangler

Gather 'round you mountain climbers and attend the
    tale I tell,
Of a Sunday not so very long ago,
When I chanced to spend the day upon the cliffs of
    Carderock
And a second time I climbed with Jam Crack Joe.

I had searched the highest summits of the Andes and
    the Alps,
Of the Tetons and Himalayan peaks galore;
But in forty years of travel I had never found my friend
Till that day upon the steep Potomac shore.

'Twas the middle of the winter, and the rocks were
    slick with ice.
I was trudging in a snowbank at their base,
When I saw a man rappelling on a length on nylon
    rope,
And I gazed into a well-remembered face.

Oh, his hair was white, his features lined, his body stooped
    with age;
On his pack a pair of crutches he had tied.
But I knew him by his clothes, he hadn't changed them
    since that day

When so long ago I scrambled at his side.

As he reached the ground beside me, oh, he slapped me
    on the back.
"Who'd have thought," he said, "that I would meet you
    here?
'Tis like yesterday that I recall our climb upon the
    ridge
And the night we spent tied up with climbing gear."

Oh, I pestered him with questions, but he only shook
    his head.
"Do not ask," he said, "the things that happened then.
I have climbed from Aconcagua to the Mountains of the
    Moon,
But I vowed that I will never climb again.

"I am tortured by lumbago and my toes are frozen off,
The high altitudes have strained my heart to death.
So I've left this mountain madness to a younger race of
    men.
Here at Carderock I'll draw my dying breath."

I was gripped by sad emotion as I listened to his words,
But his eyes were bright and happy as could be.
As he coiled his rope he told me of the wonders of the
    place,
Of the dread Crossover and the Lunacy.

Then we walked along together through the February snow,
And he pointed to a rock not very high.
"Do you see that climb?" he asked me, "'Tis the Spider
    Walk, I'm told.
It's the one thing I must do before I die."

So without a moment's pause he tied a bowline in his
    rope.

Jan Conn (Wexler)

Tenderly he laid his hands upon the cliff.
As he stuck his bony fingers deep within the crack he
    said,
"'Twould be easy if I weren't so old and stiff."

Then he swung his feet up on the face just underneath his
    hands
With his body doubled up and laying back.
How he stuck upon that icy wall is more than I can see,
But he did it with his fingers in the crack.

In this terrible position he in some way freed a hand,
And he stuck a piton in the stubborn schist,
Saying, "I have aged so much that now to pound a piton
    in,
I am forced to wear a glove upon my fist."

When his rope was running through the carabiner properly,
He climbed higher, and I held his nylon taut.
"'Twas a wicked bit of layback," and he grunted in his
    beard,
"Oh, this Spider Walk is tougher than I thought."

Then he reached his hand onto a ledge and hauled himself
    erect.
There he paused and rubbed his fingers free of ice.
With a final burst of effort he was standing on the top.
"You are next," he said. "The climb is very nice."

So I tried it, but my fingers were not equal to the cold,
And the handholds did not satisfy my hope.
I was just above his piton when quite suddenly I slipped,
And I found myself a-dangling on the rope.

"Try again," said Joe, and laughed at me, but then another
    voice
From below cut through the air just like a knife.

"At your age, this monkey business! Come along, you're
   going home.
And I knew beyond a doubt it was my wife.

So I said goodbye a second time to dear old Jam Crack
   Joe.
As he waved farewell my heart pinched like a vise.
"There are rocks on Herzog Island," were his final words
   to me.
On his crutches he was crossing on the ice.

Accident Analysis
by Stuart Pregnall

In response to an unprecedented number of climbing
accidents along the Potomac River Gorge during the 1987
climbing season, the PATC Mountaineering Section
undertook a local climbing safety analysis. It was hoped
that this safety analysis would be useful to other climbers
in that it would identify and highlight climbing practices
that might lead to future accidents. Climbers thus warned
would then refrain from these practices, and make certain
that their climbing was achieved more safely.

Over the past year (1987), the National Park Service (NPS)
has responded to no less than seven climbing accidents in
the local area. During 1986 the NPS responded to only
one accident, and the same number for 1985 and 1984.
Whereas these statistics may seem insignificant when
compared to the growing number of local climbers, it is
alarming to many of those who have climbed in the area
for several years to see the sudden increase in accidents.
What is more alarming is the severity of a couple of these
accidents. After all, it is common knowledge that top
roping is "safe."

We requested accident reports from the National Park
Service jurisdictions for Great Falls Virginia and Maryland,
and for Carderock. The Park Service was enthusiastic to
participate in this analysis, and provided adequate data
from which to draw some clear conclusions. Data were
requested on a number of accident details, including the
experience of the climbers involved, whether or not they
were climbing with an organized group, and objective
details such as weather factors that might have been

contributing factors. Further, details were sought on the degree of complexity of the rescues involved.

A total of ten accident reports were submitted by the Park Service and analyzed.

All but one accident took place on sunny, warm days. Weather was therefore excluded as a contributing factor.

Five of the accidents took place while top roping, two occurred while free soloing, two were rappeling accidents, and the last accident had no determined climbing practice identified. It is therefore clear that top roping can be dangerous (as well as soloing and rappeling) and that there is a definite need to identify the contributing causes to these top rope accidents.

Four of the climbers were in their teens, three were in their twenties, one in the thirties, and one was forty-four years of age. Not surprisingly, only one of these climbers had been climbing more than three years. It can thus be conjectured that age and experience played a role in these accidents; the less experienced climber may well be at more risk than the experienced climber.

None of the climbers were participating with organized group climbs. It is possible that control over risk factors is greater when climbing with a group since there are more people paying attention to safety details.

Two of the top rope accidents were caused by rope tie in failures. Another top rope accident occurred when the belay anchor failed--the climbers had tied into a rotten tree stump. One of the top rope accidents was caused in part by poor communications between climbers and ineffective belaying. The precise cause of the last top rope accident was not determined.

The four top rope accidents that have had identifiable causes are linked by a common denominator: the causes were directly attributable to failure of basic climbing practices. When a climber ties into the rope, the climber should always check and then re-check the knot to ensure that it is tied properly and securely. (The same is true for securing a harness to one's body.) Further, when anchoring a top rope, one must select a belay anchor that is unquestionably sound and secure. There are innumerable good anchor trees at both Great Falls and Carderock that afford safe belays for most of the top rope routes. In certain cases, routes that require particular belay anchors are noted in the guide books. Finally, lack of communication between climbers may occur on long routes, but basic climbing instruction includes education in universally accepted signals that all climbers should know and use that avoid poor communication. Even if there is a lack of communication between climbers, the belayer should at all times manage the rope as if the climber were about to fall. Attention to proper climbing practices would have meant that accidents of this nature would be significantly reduced in number, if not eliminated altogether.

Both of the two solo accidents occurred when the climbers slipped and fell. Soloing is a practice frequently seen at Carderock, and less so at Great Falls. Because of the potentially serious results of falling when soloing, this practice is not recommended. Bouldering, or soloing in reasonable proximity to the ground, permits a lone climber to practice his skill while minimizing risk. Climbers who choose to solo or boulder, however, should do so only with the knowledge that they are giving up the basic safety tool used in climbing, i.e., the rope, and that an unroped fall can have serious consequences.

Neither rappeler who was involved in an accident was experienced. Both slipped while rappeling and were injured when their bodies swung into the rock. Instruction in proper rappeling technique would have reduced the potential for these accidents. Further, as they were both beginners learning to rappel, a top rope belay would have prevented the accidents from happening.

In summary, inexperience and improper climbing practices led to the majority of the accidents analyzed. It would be proper to caution climbers who are uncertain of their climbing practices to seek instruction from experienced climbers or from one of the several groups who offer it. It would also be proper to suggest that inexperienced climbers climb with more experienced climbers until they are certain that their abilities and judgement are sufficient to safely avoid the risks inherent to climbing. The climbing community in the Washington area is quite friendly, and it is simple to join in with other climbers while top roping. In addition, there are groups that participate in climbing, of which the PATC Mountaineering Section is but one.

The PATC Mountaineering Section would like to thank the National Park Service for making sufficient information available to perform the accident risk analysis. The continued cooperation between Park officials and climbers will lead to safer enjoyment of the rock resources available to us all.

References

Conn, Herb and Arnold Wexler. 1944. "Carderock
    Climbs" PATC Bulletin, July: 59-66.

Eakin, James. 1985. *Climber's Guide to the Great Falls
    of the Potomac.* Potomac Appalachian Trail Club,
    Mountaineering Section, Washington DC.

Gregory, John C. 1980. *Carderock.* S&S Printing, Inc.,
    Chester, Vermont.

Reed, John C. Jr., R. S. Sigafoos and G.W. Fisher. 1980.
    *The River and the Rocks: The Geologic Story of Great
    Falls and The Potomac Gorge.* U.S. Geological Survey
    Bulletin 1471, U.S. Government Printing Office,
    Washington D.C.

Up Rope. Volume 1--present, 1944-1990, Potomac
    Appalachian Trail Club Mountaineering Section,
    Washington D.C.

Index

Climbs by rating

Climbs alphabetical